Entrepreneur  QUICK GUIDE

CREATING, PLANNING, and FUNDING

Entrepreneur Press, Publisher
Cover Design: Andrew Welyczko
Production and Composition: Nathaniel Roy
© 2024 by Entrepreneur Media, LLC
All rights reserved.

This publication is designed to provide accurate and authoritative information in regard to the subject matter covered. It is sold with the understanding that the publisher is not engaged in rendering legal, accounting, or other professional services. If legal advice or other expert assistance is required, the services of a competent professional person should be sought.

Entrepreneur Press® is a registered trademark of Entrepreneur Media, LLC
Library of Congress Cataloging-in-Publication Data

Names: Diamond, Stephanie, author.
Title: Creating, planning, and funding your new business / by the Staff of
  Entrepreneur Media and Stephanie Diamond.
Description: Irvine : Entrepreneur Press, [2024] | Series: Entrepreneur
  quick guide | Summary: "Creating, Planning, and Funding Your New
  Business is a comprehensive guide that will assist you in thinking,
  planning, funding, and preparing for the launch of your business"--
  Provided by publisher.
Identifiers: LCCN 2023039985 (print) | LCCN 2023039986 (ebook) | ISBN
  9781642011722 (paperback) | ISBN 9781613084779 (epub)
Subjects: LCSH: New business enterprises. | Business planning.
Classification: LCC HD62.5 .D5155 2024 (print) | LCC HD62.5 (ebook) | DDC
  658.1/1--dc23/eng/20230825
LC record available at https://lccn.loc.gov/2023039985
LC ebook record available at https://lccn.loc.gov/2023039986

Entrepreneur® QUICK GUIDE

CREATING, PLANNING, and FUNDING

Your New Business

 1 **Develop Your Start-Up Idea**

 2 **Craft A Winning Business Plan**

 3 **Secure Financing For Launch**

BY THE STAFF OF ENTREPRENEUR MEDIA AND STEPHANIE DIAMOND

CONTENTS

PART 1
Creating

CHAPTER 1
Introduction

ARE YOU READY TO TAKE THE LEAP into entrepreneurship? Before diving headfirst into creating, planning, and funding a new business, it's essential to determine whether you are ready for this exciting and challenging journey. Becoming an entrepreneur requires a unique mindset, careful planning, a clear vision, and a willingness to adapt to the ever-changing landscape of entrepreneurship. With your purchase of the *Entrepreneur Quick Guide: Creating, Planning, and Funding Your New Business*, you've taken a tangible step toward understanding and navigating this complex world.

This book is not just a theoretical overview; it's a hands-on manual designed to guide you through the early stages of starting and launching a business. It offers actionable advice and breaks it down into manageable steps. If you're new to entrepreneurship, this guide walks you through the basics to provide a solid foundation. Some of the topics covered include:

Creating

Determining whether you are ready to become an entrepreneur: One of the first steps in determining your readiness is evaluating your passion and motivation. Ask yourself if you have a burning desire to start your own business and are willing to put in the necessary time, effort, and commitment. If you are not driven and passionate about your business idea, sustaining the required level of dedication may be challenging.

Idea assessment: Before embarking on the journey of starting a new business, it is essential to evaluate your business idea. Idea assessment helps you gauge your concept's feasibility, potential, and viability, giving you confidence and direction to move forward.

Choosing full-time or part-time: Choosing whether to start a business on a full-time or part-time basis is an important decision that can significantly impact your success. While there is no one-size-fits-all answer, it is crucial to carefully consider your personal circumstances, financial situation, and level of commitment before making this choice.

Deciding whether to start or buy a business: Deciding whether to start or buy a business can be a tough decision. Starting a business allows you to pursue a passion or a unique business idea. It enables you to shape the company culture, set your goals, and build a team that shares your vision. On the other hand, buying a business may be better if you have specific industry expertise or prefer a more structured and established business model.

Planning

Defining your ideal customer: Knowing your customer is crucial in creating, planning, and funding a new business. By identifying your ideal customer, you can tailor your products or services to meet their specific needs.

Conducting market research: Market research is essential to creating, planning, and funding a new business. Entrepreneurs can make informed decisions and develop effective strategies by conducting industry analysis and understanding the target market.

Legal and regulatory compliance: Legal and regulatory compliance is critical to running a successful business. It involves ensuring that your company always operates within the boundaries of applicable laws and regulations. Failing to comply with legal requirements can result in significant fines, penalties, and even legal action, harming your business's reputation and financial stability.

Developing a winning plan: A winning business plan is not just about having all the answers, but a strategic and agile mindset. Adaptability and a willingness to learn and adjust your strategies will be key to your business's long-term success.

Funding

Working with family: Working with family can be both rewarding and challenging. On the one hand, you can work with people you know and trust, allowing for seamless communication and a shared vision. On the other hand, there can be unique dynamics and personalities at play that can make things more complex.

Finding investors: Securing funding is vital in turning your business idea into a reality; whether starting a small venture or launching a large-scale enterprise, having the necessary capital is crucial for success.

Funding options: Various options are available to entrepreneurs, from traditional bank loans to angel investors. Each option has its own set of advantages and considerations.

Exploring loans: While bank loans provide a reliable funding source, it's also worth exploring other options. Alternative lenders, such as online options, have emerged in recent years, offering more accessible and convenient loans.

Launching

Creating a professional image: Your brand is the face of your business. It encompasses your logo, website, colors, fonts, and overall aesthetic. Invest in professional graphic design services to create a visually appealing and cohesive brand identity that reflects your business values and appeals to your target audience.

Hiring employees: One of the most crucial steps in growing your business is hiring employees. As your business expands and the workload increases, hiring the right individuals can help you achieve your goals and take your company to new heights.

Tips and Warnings

Many business resources and tip boxes (see examples below) are included in this book.

AHA!

Here you will find helpful information or ideas you may not have thought of before.

TIP

This box gives you ideas on how to do something better or more efficiently, or simply how to work smarter.

WARNING

Here we remind you to heed the warnings to avoid common mistakes and pitfalls that others have made before you.

FYI

This box points you to current and often comprehensive websites that you might seek out for business information.

SAVE

Look for this box to provide valuable tips on ways you can save money during startup.

Entrepreneur Quick Guide: Creating, Planning, and Funding Your New Business is a comprehensive, practical, and up-to-date resource for anyone serious about entrepreneurship. It's a grounded guide that speaks to business ownership's real challenges and opportunities. Remember, it is more than just a purchase; it's an investment in your future. It's a resource that you can return to time and again. It's a valuable addition to any entrepreneur's tool kit, with clear instructions, actionable advice, and a realistic approach. With the knowledge and insights this guide provides, this book is your starting road map to success. Enjoy your business adventure!

CHAPTER 2
Taking the Plunge

Get Ready to Be an Entrepreneur

SOME PEOPLE WORRY WHETHER THEY HAVE WHAT IT TAKES to be an entrepreneur. If this is you, stop worrying. We firmly believe anyone with the desire and the initiative can be an entrepreneur. And since you purchased this book, it's likely you have both.

But just because you can be an entrepreneur doesn't mean that now is the right time to take the plunge. This chapter will help you determine if you're ready for entrepreneurship right now or if you should hold off for a bit.

The Entrepreneurial Personality

Every year, hundreds of thousands of people start their own businesses. But while most succeed (yes, that's the truth!), many fail. Why? One of the common causes of startup failure is lack of preparation.

People come to the entrepreneurial path from many different directions. Increasingly, some start fresh out of college (or even before graduating) while others start after a stint at home raising their kids. Others seek entrepreneurship simply because the idea of retiring is abhorrent to them. Most, though, come to entrepreneurship straight out of the workforce. And many of them have dabbled in their would-be area of business before they take the plunge completely, testing ideas on the side while maintaining a day job. There are also those that have taken jobs to learn more about an industry before jumping into it as a business owner. Quitting a full-time job to start a business isn't a decision to be taken lightly. You should be sure that now is the right time to get started. First, you need to ask yourself some important questions. First and foremost: Do you have enough money for living expenses? Can you support yourself while taking the time and effort to get a business off the ground? If you are married and/or have a family, are they ready for this? Is there a need for a product or service like yours? *The Entrepreneur Quick Guide* will help you answer those questions.

WARNING

If you have a family, discuss your plan to open a business. Explain that you will need a lot of time to work on this new aspect of your life and that you're doing it for the family. Make sure they understand the emotional and financial sacrifices business success requires. When your family doesn't support your business—if they're always saying "Can't you spend more time with us this weekend?"—it's going to be tough to make your business work. If your family isn't ready for you to become an entrepreneur, this may not be the right time.

Full Steam Ahead

Many successful entrepreneurs recall having a sense of urgency while starting out. Even though it would take them some time to get the business off the ground, it was that sense of urgency that they attribute to being their driving force. One entrepreneur's advice: "You'll know the time is right when you can honestly say 'I'll put my house, jewelry, and other personal collateral on the line to attain the startup money I need for the long-term rewards.'" We're not recommending that you put your home up as collateral, but that willingness to take major risks likely means you're ready to start now.

What's Your Impetus for Becoming an Entrepreneur?

While some people may think that one single incident—such as getting fired or being passed over for a promotion—is the impetus for becoming your own boss, most experts agree it's usually a series of desires and frustrations that leads to entrepreneurship.

A fundamental desire to control one's own destiny ranks high on most entrepreneurs' lists of reasons for starting their own businesses. This need is so strong that entrepreneurs are often willing to take many risks to be their own boss. Some people aren't able to feel truly fulfilled working for someone else; they simply cannot be happy following someone else's plan or taking orders from a boss. They're often convinced they have a better way or an idea that would revolutionize their industry—or at least their little corner of it—and working within a corporate structure is simply stifling their creativity and sense of accomplishment.

But opportunity comes in other guises too. It might be when potential customers start calling you because they've been told you're the go-to person for what they need, or perhaps a business in your area is struggling, and you know you can make it work. Or maybe you feel as if you're underemployed (working below your potential salary or your skill level) or not putting your skills and talents to their best use. Perhaps there's a need for the product or service you want to provide, or you've simply figured out a better or new way to do something. Perhaps you've simply had a passion for something for years, such as cooking, and that passion drives you to open your own restaurant.

Business Startups: By the Numbers

Why do people start businesses?

- Ready to be my own boss: 26 percent
- Pursue a passion: 23 percent
- Opportunity presented itself: 19 percent
- Dissatisfaction with corporate America: 27 percent increase in 2019

Why do businesses fail?

- No market need (idea/solution to a problem that exists): 42 percent
- Ran out of cash (poor money management): 29 percent
- Not having the right team: 23 percent

Reality Check

Once you've made the decision to break away, there are several things you should do before taking the next step. Conducting thorough market research is a must. You also need to make sure you have enough cash—not only for the business, but also to sustain your life—and discuss the decision with your family.

Remember, the rewards of small business ownership are not instantaneous. You must be determined, patient, persistent, and willing to make sacrifices to ensure those rewards eventually come.

You'll need to prepare for the responsibilities that come with business ownership. When things go wrong, the buck stops with you. You won't have the luxury of going home at 5 o'clock while the boss stays all night to fix a chaotic situation. Someone whose only desire is to get rich quick probably won't last long owning their own business.

Through surveys and research, we know that successful entrepreneurs share some common personality traits, the most important of which is *confidence*. They possess confidence not only in themselves, but also in their ability to sell their ideas, set up a business, and trust their intuition along the way. The business world is fiercely competitive, and it's the entrepreneurs with confidence who survive.

FYI

Need inspiration? Check out www.ted.com/talks for inspirational speeches on almost any topic. While the site's subject matter covers everything from fitness to raising kids, its target audience is anybody with an entrepreneurial spirit. Speakers of all kinds—including many entrepreneurs—offer new ideas, inspiring thoughts, and powerful motivation you can use to empower yourself to reach new heights.

Your Strengths and Weaknesses

It's rare that one person possesses all the qualities needed to be successful in business. Everyone has strong suits and weak points. What's important is to understand your strengths and weaknesses. To do this, you need to evaluate your skills, including those you have used to reach major achievements in your personal and professional life and those that you have not yet put to the test. The following steps can help:

- *Take a personal inventory.* Start by listing the skills you have used successfully at your various jobs. Put a check next to the areas in which you excelled and circle those that you also enjoyed the most. If it helps, keep your resume handy so you don't forget any of your past positions— today people move around often, so it's possible to forget those five days at Fred's Furniture or some other company.

  Next, add the other skills you have used at school, in associations or organizations to which you belonged, or simply in your personal life. Many of us have skills that we never use at work. Perhaps you devote a lot of time and effort to a hobby, and you have developed great organizational skills from that pursuit. Again, circle the skills that you enjoyed using the most.

Now you have an idea of what skills you have performed often and which ones you enjoyed using.

- *Analyze your personal attributes.* Are you friendly and self-motivated? A hard worker? Well organized? Evaluating your personal attributes reveals your strengths and weaknesses. If you don't feel comfortable around other people, for example, that's OK. While businesses typically require interaction with customers, there are businesses in which you do not have to be the one doing the interacting. Many people design and create new products, but they don't often interact with the people buying those products. Moreover, if you start a business in the digital world, you need not be a "people person" to run a successful venture. You can always hire a "people person" to handle customer service.

- *Analyze your professional attributes.* Small business owners wear many different hats, but that doesn't mean you have to be a jack-of-all-trades. Just be aware of the areas in which you're competent and those in which you need help, such as sales, marketing, advertising, and administration. It's like the old saying: "Know what you don't know." Next to each function, record your competency level—excellent, good, fair, or poor. A few fair and poor responses do not mean you aren't up for it—it just means these are the areas in which you will need to gain expertise or find someone to help you. From day one on your entrepreneurial journey, keep in mind that in this day and age it is rare to find someone who doesn't seek help when it comes to starting a business. Whether that means teaming up with a partner, hiring employees early on, or finding a mentor, even solopreneurs find the help they need.

FYI

On Meetup.com, there are more than 30,000 groups with over 20 million members worldwide dedicated to entrepreneurship. That number has more than quadrupled in just five years. Find one that suits you at meetup.com/topics/entrepreneurship. Then join a group and "meet up" for entrepreneurial events, networking, support, and even socializing. You'll also find more than 4,000 groups related to entrepreneurship on LinkedIn—some are general, but many are more segmented, including by industry, region, and goals. Find groups that match your needs, and you can begin to interact with like-minded entrepreneurs.

Go for the Goal

In addition to evaluating your strengths and weaknesses, it's important to define your business goals. For some people, the goal is the freedom to do what they want when they want without anyone telling them otherwise. For others, the goal is simply financial security.

TIP

Once you understand your strengths and weaknesses, there are three ways to deal with them: (1) You can either improve in the areas where you are weak (by taking a class in bookkeeping, for example), (2) hire an employee to handle these aspects of the business (for instance, hiring a bookkeeper), or (3) outsource the tasks (such as contracting an outside company to do your bookkeeping). Outsourcing small tasks and one-off assignments to experts at reasonable rates has become much simpler with formal work-for-hire freelancer websites like Upwork.com or Guru.com. There is also a great movement toward DIY (do it yourself) with websites, podcasts, software, apps, and other information sources from which you can learn to handle a lot of tasks on your own.

Setting goals is an integral part of choosing the business that's right for you. After all, if your business doesn't meet your personal goals, you probably won't be happy waking up each morning and trying to make the business a success. Sooner or later, you'll stop putting forth the effort needed to make the concept work. When setting goals, aim for the following qualities:

- *Practicality/realism.* Those who thought Rome would be built in a day weren't being practical or realistic. You need to set practical and realistic goals. If, for example, you set a goal to earn $100,000 a month when you've never earned that much in a year, that goal is unrealistic. Begin with small steps, such as increasing your monthly income by 25 percent. Once your first goal is met, you can reach for larger ones.

  Keep in mind that you also want to set both realistic short- and long-term goals. Short-term goals are attainable in a period of weeks or months, perhaps a year. Long-term goals can be for five, 10, or even 20 years; they should be substantially greater than short-term goals but should still be realistic.

From the Horse's Mouth

One of the best ways to determine if now is the best time to start a business is to meet with other entrepreneurs, those who have been at it a while. This way you can get a better grasp of what they do and how they do it. It's not about their specific products or services but about how they run a business. Looking at their lives and talking about entrepreneurship can help you figure out if you're ready.

Often, when you talk to someone who's done it, they'll tell you all the negative things about owning a business, like the time they had to work a 24-hour day or when the power went out right as they were trying to meet a huge deadline. But those are the things you need to hear about before you get started.

In addition to meeting with successful entrepreneurs, you might want to talk to a few who weren't so successful. They may be harder to locate, but sometimes you'll find an entrepreneur who is on their second or third business and one or two didn't work out as they would have liked. Find out what happened with their previous attempts. You can learn from other people's adventures. Sometimes the business failed; other times they had loftier goals than a particular business could allow them to reach. Whatever their stories are, you can learn something.

Many potential business owners also find it useful to attend entrepreneurial seminars or classes. You can often find such courses at community colleges, continuing education programs near you, or online. Others seek assistance from consulting firms that specialize in helping small businesses get off the ground. Associations and organizations, both private and public, such as SCORE or Small Business Development Centers, or your local chamber of commerce, may be eager to assist you. Don't hesitate to ask for assistance. Most experienced entrepreneurs enjoy helping newcomers like you succeed.

Should You Go Solo?

Solopreneurs are a powerful and growing force in today's career landscape. A *solopreneur* is a business owner who works and runs their business alone. A solopreneur is also the proverbial chief cook and bottle washer, who started the business, owns the business, runs the business, and is responsible for its failure or success. The benefits of solopreneurship are better experienced than reported. If you're curious about the lives of these disentangled, high-risk, high-reward captains of their own fate and are considering taking the same plunge, here's what you can expect:

1.   You work long hours. Starting a business on your own takes an ongoing time commitment. This means pouring your heart and soul into the business and often putting in 60- or 70-hour weeks.

2. You make personal sacrifices. You may have to sacrifice some time with your spouse, your significant other, and/or your kids, which is difficult, but at least you will have a built-in excuse to get out of dinners with distant relatives who can't wait to see you to roll their eyes at your business ideas. Personal sacrifices are not easy, but if you are dedicated to reaching your goal, let others know such sacrifices are for a good reason.

3. You get to hire the personnel you want. Most solopreneurs aren't 100 percent on their own. They hire people. They manage people. They even get to boss people around, sort of. The process, however, is different. Instead of employing a CFO, the solopreneur might engage the services of advisors or work with contractors. You get to figure out what kind of help you need and find the best people to work with you.

4. You get to make the big decisions. From the company name and whether to have a company logo to the decision to work remotely or have an office or several stores, you get to make the decisions. This isn't to say you can't get advice on all these and other important matters—it's perfectly OK to seek help when making such decisions.

5. You get to create the processes rather than someone telling you how things will get done. From manual labor to automation to the latest in virtual and AI technology, how you will build the perfect state-of-the-art widget is up to you.

6. You'll be able to pivot when necessary. If the proverbial ship is heading for an iceberg, it's up to you to pivot and take a new course. Pivots are a survival tactic; being in charge means you can choose to stop on a dime and make a change. Solopreneurs pivot too, and they can do so without any accountability to shareholders, stakeholders, board members, or even a pet cat. They can pivot like nobody's business.

7. You create the schedule(s). Do you want to work 9-to-5, 5-to-9, or 9-to-9? You can decide when you're open and when you're closed. You can decide on full-time hours, part-time hours, flex hours, and so on. You're the one in charge—deciding how, when, where, and how long to work is completely up to you. Most solopreneurs, however, find their day extending beyond their plans because there's so much to get done, even after hiring some help.

8. You are responsible for your own success. You have to take big risks if you want big rewards. Solopreneurs internalize this truth. Rather than leave their success to the whimsy of an employer, they choose to take their success firmly in hand.

9. You get to develop your own vision. A solopreneur makes this decision with fierce independence and experiences true fulfill-ment as a result.

10. You get to embody your own brand and that of your business. Branding is the practice of creating and curating the public identity of your business.

11. You get to keep what you make. You're no longer making money for the owners of the company—you're the owner. Of course, you will still have to pay taxes. Quite a bit, actually. On the other hand, your business profits are yours. You can choose to incorporate as an LLC or an S corp, but either way, the money your business makes is the money that you make. Invest wisely.

12. You experience adventure every day. An adventure is defined as "an unusual and exciting, often risky experience or activity." That basically sums up solopreneurship. Job security? Not a chance. Steady paycheck? Nope. Benefits? You're kidding. You live a life of adrenaline-pumping adventure, and if you are truly cut out to be an entrepreneur, you wouldn't have it any other way.

13. The life of a solopreneur, or entrepreneur, is not for everyone. The risks are high. The burdens and sacrifices are great. But the experience is transformative.

- *Specificity.* You have a better chance of achieving a goal if it's specific. "Raising capital" isn't a specific goal; "raising $10,000 by July 1" is.
- *Optimism.* Be positive when you set your goals. "Being able to pay the bills" isn't exactly an inspirational goal. "Achieving financial security" phrases your goal in a more positive manner, thus firing up your energy to attain it.

Consider several factors when setting your goals:

- *Income.* Many entrepreneurs go into business to achieve financial security. Consider how much money you want to make during your first year of operation and each year thereafter, up to five years.
- *Lifestyle.* This includes areas such as travel, work hours, personal asset investments, and geographic location. Are you willing to travel extensively or move? How many hours are you willing to work? Which assets are you willing to risk?
- *Type of work.* When setting goals for type of work, you need to determine whether you like working outdoors, in an office, with computers, on the phone, with lots of people, with children, and so on.
- *Ego gratification.* Face it: Many people go into business to satisfy their egos. Owning a business can be very ego-gratifying. You need to decide how important ego gratification is to you and what business best fills that need.

The most important rule of self-evaluation and goal-setting is *honesty.* Going into business with your eyes wide open about your strengths and weaknesses, your likes and dislikes, and your ultimate goals lets you confront the decisions you'll face with more confidence and a greater chance of success.

FYI

The SBA Women's Business Center has a lot to offer women—and men too—from answering questions about financing businesses or becoming an international company to finding a mentor. Search online for SBA Women's Business Center to find centers near you.

CHAPTER 3
Good Idea!

How Do I Know If I Have a Great Idea for a Business?

MANY PEOPLE BELIEVE STARTING A BUSINESS is a mysterious process. They know they want to start a business, but they don't know the first steps to take. In this chapter, you're going to find out whether a business idea you already have is a viable one. If it's not, we will take you through the steps to finding a feasible business idea, then show you how to take action on it. This is the biggest step in figuring out what it is you want to do.

But before we get started, let's clear up one point: People always wonder if this is a good time to start their business. The fact is there's never a bad time to launch a business. It's obvious why it's smart to launch in strong economic times. People have money and are looking for ways to spend it. But launching in tough or uncertain economic times can be just as smart. If you do your homework, presumably there's a need for the business you're starting. Because many people are reluctant to launch in tough times, your new business has a better chance of getting noticed. And, depending on your idea, in a down economy there is often equipment (or even entire businesses!) for sale at bargain prices.

Estimates vary, but according to data from the U.S. Census Bureau, over five million new businesses were started in 2022. Yet for every American who starts a business, there are likely millions more who begin each year saying "OK, this is the year I am going to start a business," and then don't.

Everyone has their own roadblock, something that prevents them from taking that crucial first step. Most people are afraid to start; they may fear the unknown, failure, or even success. Others find starting something overwhelming because they think they have to come up with something that no one has ever done before—a new invention, a unique service. In other words, they think they have to reinvent the wheel.

For most people starting a business, the issue should not be coming up with something so unique that no one has ever heard of it but instead answering the questions: How can I improve on this? Or "Can I find a new way to build something, improve on an existing product, find a new means of selling or shipping items, or improve on an already great idea? After all, Henry Ford did not invent the automobile; he simply figured out how to make it affordable enough so that the masses could buy them. For that matter, Bill Gates did not invent the computer, he just revolutionized it in ways we had previously not imagined. You can also ask: Is there a pain point for consumers, and can I find a solution for them? Or simply, is there market share not being served that makes room for another business in this category? Most new businesses are not discovering uncharted territory or selling products that are new inventions, instead they are finding new ways to use and mine that territory.

"Even if you don't have the perfect idea to begin with, you can likely adapt."
—Victoria Ransom, cofounder of Wildfire Interactive

Get the Juices Flowing

If you don't have a specific business idea, but you know that you would love the idea of having your own business, start thinking about what type of business you would most enjoy starting. It should be something you feel good about, something that would be fulfilling and personally gratifying. After all, if you are not passionate about your business idea, it will be difficult to spend numerous hours and make major sacrifices to make a go of it.

So, how do you start the idea process? First, take out a sheet of paper, or open a new file on your computer, and across the top write "Things About Me." Then, list five to seven things about yourself—things you like to do or that you're really good at, personal things (we'll get to your work life in a minute). Your list might include "I'm really good with people, I love kids, I love to read, I love computers, I love numbers, I'm good at coming up with marketing concepts, I'm a problem solver." Just write down whatever comes to your mind; it doesn't need to make sense. Once you have your list, number the items down one side of the paper.

On the other side of the paper, list things you don't think you're good at or you don't like to do. Maybe you're really good at marketing concepts, but you don't like to meet people, or you're really not that fond of kids, or you don't like to do public speaking, or you don't want to travel. Don't overthink it.

When you're finished, ask yourself: "If there were three to five products or services that would make my personal life better, what would they be?" This is your personal life as a man, woman, father, husband, mother, wife, parent, grandparent—whatever your situation may be. Determine what products or services would make your life easier or happier, make you more productive or efficient, or simply give you more time.

Next, ask yourself the same questions about your business life. Examine what you like and dislike about your work life, as well as what traits people like and dislike about you. What could you do to make your work life easier? How could you improve on the way things are done in your industry? Don't worry if you do not have instant answers. Just start exploring the world around you more closely.

Now think about your neighborhood, community, town, or city. What is missing you think people need? Is there an under-served market of interest? Is your town missing a family-friendly restaurant? A car wash? A spa? Is there a service you think is missing? Remember, a business doesn't have to be based on a new invention; it just needs to solve the needs of your community, be it a town of 2,000 people or a city of 2 million.

Finally, ask yourself why you're starting a business in the first place. Then when you're done, look for a pattern (that is, whether there's a need for a business doing one of the things you like or are good at).

TIP

Along with checking out websites, don't overlook publications in your search for business ideas. Books, newspapers, and magazines all contain a wealth of ideas. Your reading list should include business, lifestyle, and niche publications like pets or antique tractors. Read your local newspaper, as well as major newspapers from the large trendsetting cities like Los Angeles, New York, and San Francisco. You can still find many newspapers and magazines online for free, while others may be worth the cost of a subscription.

AHA!

Your hobbies may also lead you to business ideas. If gardening or antique toy collecting are what interests you, take your passion and turn it into a real business. Sell your locally grown herbs or vegetables to restaurants or set up an online business selling your rare toy finds on eBay or on your own website. Hobbies also lead to magazines, popular websites, blogs, and podcasts, which can generate advertising and/or subscriptions.

Inspiring Moments

Inspiration can be anywhere. Here's another classic startup story: Before the days of on-demand movies from cable providers, did you ever get charged a fee for returning a video late? Bet you didn't do anything about it. Well, when Reed Hastings got a whopping $40 late charge, instead of getting mad, he got inspired. Hastings wondered, "How come movie rentals don't work like a health club, where whether you use it a lot or a little, you get charged the same?" From this thought, Netflix was born. From its start in 1999, Netflix has grown into a big business with revenues topping over $31.6 billion in 2022.

Getting an idea can be as simple as keeping your eyes peeled for the latest hot businesses; they crop up all the time. Many local entrepreneurs made tons of money bringing the Starbucks coffeehouse concept to their hometowns, then expanding. Take Minneapolis-based Caribou Coffee. The founders had what they describe as an "aha moment" in 1990, and two years later launched what has become one of the nation's largest corporate-owned gourmet coffeehouse chains. Other coffee entrepreneurs have chosen to stay local.

"Don't start a company unless it's an obsession and something you love. If you have an exit strategy, it's not an obsession."
                    —Mark Cuban, Serial Entrepreneur and Investor

"Plan your hunches and use your head."
                    —Lillian Vernon, founder of Lillian Vernon Corp.

Just Do It!

Hopefully by now, the process of determining what business is right for you has at least been somewhat demystified. Truth is, starting a business isn't rocket science. No, it isn't easy to begin a business, but it's not as complicated or as scary as many people think either. It's a step-by-step process that takes plenty of research, lots of determination, a healthy amount of passion, and many hours of dedication. So take it a step at a time. First step: Figure out what you want to do. Once you have the idea, talk to people to find out what they think. Ask them "Would you buy and/or use this, and how much would you pay?"

AHA!
Is there a household chore or annoyance that drives you up the wall? Common sources of frustration or irritation are great idea generators. The woman who invented the now-ubiquitous spill-proof Snack-Trap for small children (they can reach their little hands in to grab a treat, but no matter how much they shake or drop the snack cup, nothing falls out—usually) was simply tired of cleaning up Cheerios from the floor, amid the couch cushions, and in the crevices of her toddler's car seat.

Understand that many people around you won't encourage you (some will even discourage you) to pursue your entrepreneurial journey. Some will tell you they have your best interests at heart; they just want you to see the reality of the situation. Others will resent you for having the guts to follow your dream. You can't allow these naysayers to dissuade you, to stop your journey before it even begins.

In fact, once you get an idea for a business, what's the most important trait you need as an entrepreneur? Perseverance. When you set out to launch your business, you'll be told "no" more times than you ever have. You can't take it personally. It's a numbers game, and most successful entrepreneurs struggle before everything falls into place. You've got to get beyond the "no's" and move on to the next person—because eventually, you're going to get a "yes."

One of the most common warnings you'll hear is about the risk involved in starting a business. Among the risks of starting a business is the financial risk that comes with giving up a steady paycheck. You can mitigate this risk to some degree by maintaining connections in your field, which may enable you to come back to a job if all else fails. Don't give up your network or delete your contact list.

In many cases people start their new businesses on nights and weekends while still maintaining their day jobs (sometimes with fewer hours). For example, Sara Blakely developed Spanx for several years while keeping her full-time job selling fax machines; Phil Knight was an accountant selling shoes on the side for five years before fully launching Nike; Minecraft's developer, Markus Persson, was a programmer who built games on the side and kept his day job for a full year before committing to Minecraft full time. We'll talk more about juggling a job and a business in the next chapter.

We'll talk more about funding your business later in the book, but suffice to say, you will usually need to have some funding set aside that you can use to put into your business. Other risks that factor into starting a business include competitive, market, political, environmental, and economic risks. While many risks are out of your control, you need to be aware of them and even address them in your business plan (which we'll also cover later).

Bottom line, starting a business comes with risk, and people will constantly remind you of that. But success is almost always predicated with a fair amount of risk. In this case you want to take calculated risks as opposed to foolish ones. You can mitigate your risk if you carefully consider what you're doing, get help when you need it, learn as much as you can about the business/industry, and never stop asking questions.

If you still have concerns about risk, take some time to do a self-assessment of your risk tolerance. Not everyone feels comfortable with the same level of risk—and that's OK. Start by asking yourself: What am I really risking? What am I giving up? What will I lose if things don't work out? That's the biggest concern when it comes to risk: Can you tolerate the results if they are not favorable, and then move forward understanding that you took a chance?

The most important concern when risk taking is that you don't risk what you can't afford: your home, your family, or your health.

Fit to a "T"

Every year in *Entrepreneur*, the hottest business trends for the coming year are profiled, representing a lot of research and a lot of homework. But that doesn't mean these businesses will work for you. After all, you may not be interested in these opportunities, or you may be living in an area where there are plenty of similar ventures. Conversely, a business simply may not be viable in your area or region of the country. For example, you probably won't sell a lot of snowmobiles in Miami. Get to know the latest business trends and determine which ones are of interest to you and are viable in your neck of the woods. However, if you see an opportunity that really suits you, remember that you can always go the online business route, which means you can sell products or services anywhere to anyone.

CHAPTER 4
Good Timing

Should You Launch Your Business Part or Full Time?

SHOULD YOU START YOUR BUSINESS part time or full time? Even if you ultimately plan to go full time, many entrepreneurs and experts say starting part time can be a good idea.

Starting part time offers several advantages. As noted in the previous chapter, it reduces your risk because you can rely on income and benefits from your full-time job. Starting part time also allows your business to grow gradually.

Yet, the part-time path is not without its own dangers and disadvantages. Starting part time leaves you with less time to market your own business, strategize, and build a clientele. Because you won't be available to answer calls or solve customers' problems for most of the day, clients may become frustrated and feel you're not offering adequate customer service or responding quickly enough to their needs.

Perhaps the biggest problem for part-time entrepreneurs is the risk of burnout. Holding down a full-time job while running a part-time business leaves you with little, if any, leisure time; as a result, your personal and family life may suffer.

That's not to say a part-time business can't work. It can, if you have excellent time management skills, strong self-discipline, and support from family and friends. Also, crucially, don't think that since you already have a job, you don't really have to work hard at your business.

Market Matters

As with any business, your plan of attack should start with a thorough assessment of your idea's market potential. Often, this step alone will be enough to tell you whether you should start part time or full time or shift gears to a different idea altogether.

You don't want to be married to one idea so much that you have blinders on when it comes to the realities of success. If you find there is a huge unmet need for your product or service, no major competition, and a ready supply of eager customers, then by all means go ahead and start full time. If, on the other hand, you find that the market won't support a full-time business but might someday with proper marketing and business development, then it is probably best to start part time. There are several investigative factors to consider, such as the competition in your industry, the economy in your area, the demographic breakdown of your client base, and the availability of potential customers. If you are thinking of opening an upscale beauty salon, for example, evaluate the number of similar shops in operation, as well as the number of affluent women in the area and the fees they are willing to pay.

In some cases, you might find there is no competition, which initially seems like a good thing. However, you may find out that others have tried and failed at your business idea. When there's no competition, there's often a reason why, which could be anything from zoning laws to technology that has replaced the need for your business, such as print shops. So if you find no one in your business space, keep researching to figure out why. While it's possible that you have a unique idea, that's not usually the case. A little competition usually means you're on the right track.

Once you have determined there is a need for your business, outline your goals and strategies in a comprehensive business plan. You should always conduct extensive research, make market projections for your business, and set goals for yourself based on these findings. A business plan gives you a tremendous view of the long-range possibilities and keeps the business on the right track. Don't neglect writing a business plan even if you're starting part time; a well-written business plan will help you take your business full time later on.

Certain businesses lend themselves well to part-time operation: ecommerce, direct marketing, and service businesses are examples. Doing your market research and business plan will give you a more realistic idea of whether your business can work part time.

If you've got your heart set on a business that traditionally requires a full-time commitment, think creatively; there may be ways to make it work on a part-time basis. For instance, instead of a restaurant, consider a catering business. You'll still get to create menus and interact with customers, but your work can all be done during evenings and weekends. Or if you want to start a graphic design business, take on just one or two clients. You'll build your portfolio but will be able to manage your work around your other commitments. And as a bonus, as would-be clients come your way, you'll have a good sense of how long tasks take. You'll also be in a good position to understand how much you can take on when you tackle your business full time.

WARNING
Don't bite the hand that feeds you. Starting a business that competes with your current employer may get you in legal hot water by violating noncompete clauses in your employment contract. Moreover, don't poach employees from your current company unless you really want to invite legal disputes.

Financial Plan

One major factor in the decision to start part time or full time is your financial situation. Before launching a full-time business, most experts recommend putting aside enough to live on for at least six months to a year.

Basic factors you should consider include the amount of your existing savings, whether you have assets that could be sold for cash, whether friends or family members might offer you financing or loans, and whether your spouse or other family members' salaries could be enough to support your family while you launch a business full time.

If, like many people, you lack the financial resources to start full time, beginning part time is often a good alternative. However, even if you do start part time, you'll want to keep some figures in mind: Specifically, how do you know when your business is making enough money that you can say goodbye to your day job? You might also realize that you want to stay part time because you don't think you would enjoy, or profit enough, from taking the business full time. In some cases, people have run part-time businesses just long enough to realize they don't like it. Hopefully, this will not be the case, but it does happen.

A good rule of thumb is to wait until your part-time business is bringing in the income equivalent to at least 30 percent of your current salary from your full-time job. Another good idea: Start putting more money aside while you still have your day job. That way, when you take the full-time plunge, you'll have a financial cushion to supplement the income from your business.

AHA!

If keeping a full-time job and a part-time business going at the same time sounds too difficult, and taking the full-time plunge sounds too scary, consider taking a part-time or temporary job while you start a full-time business. This can be a way to ensure you have some salary coming in while giving you time to work on your business. Part-time jobs often offer evening or weekend hours—a big plus if you need to be accessible to clients during regular business hours. There may also be jobs that you can walk away from at the end of each day without having to think much about them. For example, some young entrepreneurs take on bartending or a front-desk position at a local gym just to bring in some cash while keeping their mental focus on their new business. Often, the more routine the job is, the more it allows you to concentrate your efforts on your new business endeavor.

Family Affairs

The emotional and psychological side of starting a business is less cut-and-dried than financial and market aspects, but it's just as important in your decision to start part time or full time.

Begin by discussing the situation with your spouse, significant other, or family members. Do they support your decision to start a business? Do they understand the sacrifices both full-time and part-time businesses will require—from you, from them, and from the whole family? Make sure your loved ones feel free to bring any objections or worries out in the open. The time to do this is now—not three months after you have committed to your business and it is too late to back out.

After agreeing on what sacrifices can and will be made, work together to come up with practical solutions to the problems you foresee. Could your spouse take over some of the household chores you handle? Lay some ground rules for the part-time business—for instance, no work on Sunday afternoons or no discussing business at the dinner table.

To make your part-time business a success and keep your family happy, time management is key. Balance the hours you have available. Get up early, and don't spend valuable time on frivolous phone calls and other time wasters.

Bring Everyone Along: The Family Business

According to the Conway Center for Family Business, 64 percent of U.S. gross national product comes from family businesses. In fact, 35 percent of Fortune 500 companies are family controlled. In short, family-owned and/or -run businesses comprise a significant percentage of all the companies in the United States and have for decades. You'll notice many family members running local shops and others with their names listed as founders of major corporations.

A family business may mean the company was started and/or run by a husband and wife, brothers, sisters, or the whole family. Some have been passed down for generations. In fact, family-run businesses have deep roots worldwide. The oldest family-run business is a Japanese hotel called Houshi Ryokan, which has been run by the same family since the year 718. It's safe to assume that this small inn off the west coast of Japan has had several renovations over the past 1,300-plus years!

Family-owned ventures have several advantages. For one, they can bring family members together on a shared project or mission—running the business. Close-knit family members are also able to put in the extra effort it takes to start and run a business. This is typically because they have a strong commitment and personal loyalty to one another. During downtimes (which occur in any business), families are more likely to stick together and do what is necessary to keep the business going. There is also a sense of stability since a business can continue from generation to generation. And if young family members are interested, they can learn the business as they grow up, which means they are more likely to be engaged as they become more involved at a later age.

Among the most successful family-owned businesses in the United States are Berkshire Hathaway, Ford Motor Co., Walmart, Cargill, Dell Technologies, Mars, Tyson Foods, Koch Industries, Comcast, Nike, Penske Corp., and many, many small businesses all over the country.

The flip side of family business harmony is that family members may take on roles for which they lack skills and experience. This can lead to stress and tension. Issues such as sibling rivalry and favoritism may also cause conflict among the family and trouble for the business. Moreover, some family members may not want to be a part of the business, nor are they looking to inherit it one day. And in some cases, the needs of the business may interfere with the needs of the family—and this can prove disastrous.

According to the folks at SCORE, family businesses employ 60 percent of the American workforce. Not only that, but family-owned ventures are also found in all parts of the country and in numerous industries.

What are the secrets to a successful family business? Startup-Nation offers the following 12 keys to a well-oiled family business:

1. Set some boundaries.
2. Establish clear and regular methods of communication.
3. Divide roles and responsibilities.
4. Treat it like a business.
5. Recognize the advantages of family ownership.
6. Treat family members fairly.
7. Put business relationships in writing.
8. Don't provide "sympathy" jobs for family members.
9. Draw clear management lines.
10. Seek outside advice.
11. Develop a succession plan.
12. Require outside experience first (that is, family members take classes to learn about their role in the business; for example, whomever you choose as bookkeeper should take a bookkeeping course).

Family members in business together can bond and have great experiences. It's all about communicating, sharing the same goal, and not letting the business interfere with your personal relationships. That means knowing when not to talk about the business and understanding everyone's role within the company and their commitment: Some family members may have more time to commit, while others, perhaps in college, may not have the same time to offer. It's not always easy, but it can work out very well for everyone involved. And remember, not every family member may want to be in the family business—and that's OK too.

Take It Easy

Does all work and no play make entrepreneurship no fun? Some entrepreneurs who run part-time businesses based on hobbies, such as crafts or cooking, find that going full time takes all the fun out of the venture. "Going full time turns an adventure into a job," as business expert Arnold Sanow puts it. Some entrepreneurs have trouble grasping the fact that their businesses aren't just pastimes anymore. They can't work at their leisure any longer, and their ventures may require them to develop talents they didn't know they had and perform tasks they'd rather leave to someone else. Don't get so caught up in the creative aspects of the venture that you lose sight of the business responsibilities you must assume to make your startup succeed. Take a realistic look at what going full time will require. Consider hiring people to handle the business aspects you dislike, such as sales or operations, but keep tabs on whatever they are doing so you can be sure it benefits the business.

Getting Personal

If the idea of taking the full-time business plunge and giving up your comfy salary and cushy benefits keeps you awake at night biting your nails, then perhaps a part-time business is best. On the other hand, if you need to work long hours at your current full-time job, you commute 60 miles round trip, and you have two-year-old

triplets, piling a part-time business on top of all those commitments could be the straw that breaks the camel's back.

Starting a full-time business requires long hours, but a part-
time business combined with a full-time job can be even more
stressful. If this is the route you're considering, carefully assess
the effects it could have on your life. You'll be using evenings,
weekends, and lunch hours—and, most likely, your holidays, sick
days, and vacation time—to take care of business. You'll probably
have to give up leisure activities, such as bingeing your favorite
TV shows, reading, hiking, biking, or dining out often. How will
you feel the next time you drag yourself home, exhausted after
a late night at the office, then have to sit right down and spend
four hours working on a project that a client needs the next
morning? Carefully consider whether you have the mental and
physical stamina to give your best effort to both your job and
your business.

TIP

What do you do if you can't afford to start your business full time but
need to be available full time to answer client and customer calls?
Consider teaming up with a partner whose available hours complement
yours. Or hire a freelancer to take incoming calls, answer simple questions, bring important ones to your attention, and basically hold down
the fort while you are at work. You could arrange to pay a flat fee or a
fee plus a little extra bonus for handling customer issues successfully.

Part Time Online Doesn't Mean Less Time

While some entrepreneurs are still opening brick-and-mortar operations, many are choosing to start part-time online businesses. DIY-style sites like Etsy allow people in creative fields to launch without the commitment of even having their own online store. And eBay remains a platform for those in retail to set up shop online (exclusively or otherwise). Setting up an online order–based business—or any business for that matter—that you intend to run part time can be a quick, easy, and less costly way to begin. But it isn't necessarily less time intensive.

For instance, if you start an Etsy shop and one day hope to turn your organic cotton T-shirt business into a full-time venture, you'll need to spend time on marketing your goods, perfecting your search engine optimization, building your brand and social media presence, and, of course, regularly adding and creating new products to sell. You'll also need to fulfill orders and consider how you might scale the business if you need to. The same is true if you're starting a resume or college placement consulting service online. You'll need to market, manage social interactions, regularly create new products and/or services, and provide real testimonials from satisfied clients or customers.

An online business doesn't have to be full-time work, but just because it's online doesn't mean it's any less crucial to pay attention and put in the time. For more information on starting an Etsy business, check out *Start Your Own Etsy Business* (Entrepreneur Press, 2017).

CHAPTER 5
Build It or Buy It?

Starting a Business versus Buying One

WHEN MOST PEOPLE THINK OF STARTING A BUSINESS, they think of beginning from scratch—developing your own idea and building the company from the ground up. But starting from scratch presents some distinct disadvantages, including the difficulty of building a customer base, marketing the new business, hiring employees, and establishing cash flow . . . all without a track record or reputation to go on.

Some people know they want to own their own business but aren't sure exactly what type of business to choose. If you fall into this category, or if you are worried about the difficulties involved in starting a business from the ground up, the good news is that there are other options: buying an existing business, buying a franchise, or buying a business opportunity. Depending on your personality, skills, and resources, these three methods of getting into business may offer significant advantages over starting from scratch.

Buying an Existing Business

In most cases, buying an existing business is less risky than starting from scratch. When you buy a business, you can take over an operation that's already generating cash flow and profits. You have an established customer base and reputation, as well as employees who are familiar with all aspects of the business. And you do not have to reinvent the wheel—setting up new procedures, systems, and policies—since a successful formula for running the business has already been put in place.

On the downside, buying a business is often costlier than starting from scratch. However, it's often easier to get financing to buy an existing business if it has a good reputation. Bankers and investors generally feel more comfortable dealing with a business that already has a proven track record. In addition, buying a business may give you valuable legal rights, such as patents or copyrights, which can prove profitable.

Of course, there's no such thing as a sure thing—and buying an existing business is no exception. If you're not careful, you could get stuck with obsolete inventory, uncooperative employees, outdated distribution methods, yesterday's technology, and a pile of outstanding debt. To make sure you get the best deal when buying an existing business, take the following steps.

FYI

If you're looking for a business to buy or a broker to help you in your purchase, stop by BizBuySell.com. In addition to searching 45,000 businesses for sale and broker listings, you can order business valuation reports or research franchises. There are also forums and member Q&As about buying and selling a business. You might find many of your questions already asked by other would-be entrepreneurs and answered by those already in the know.

The Right Choice

Buying the perfect business starts with choosing the right type of business for you. The best place to start is by looking in an industry you are familiar with and understand. Think long and hard about the types of businesses you are interested in and which are the best matches with your skills and experience. Also consider the size of business you are looking for in terms of employees, number of locations, and sales.

Taxing Matters

You are investigating a business you like, and the seller hands you income tax returns that show a $50,000 profit. "Of course," he says with a wink and a nudge, "I really made $150,000." What do you do?

There may be perfectly legal reasons for the lower reported income. For instance, if the seller gave his nephew a nonessential job for $25,000 a year, you could just eliminate the job and keep the cash. Same goes for a fancy leased car. One-time costs of construction or equipment may have legitimately lowered net profits too.

What to watch for: a situation where a seller claims they made money but didn't report it to the IRS. If this happens, either walk away from the deal, or make an offer based on the proven income, then expect to clean up the balance sheet going forward when you take over. Either way, be careful, since in a couple of years the IRS may want to audit you over back taxes. If you're now the owner and the previous owner is nowhere to be found, you may be looking at a major expense.

Once you've chosen a region and an industry to focus on, investigate every business in the area that meets your requirements. Start by looking at websites, such as BusinessBroker.net, BizBuySell.com, or LoopNet.com. You can also look under "Business Opportunities" or "Businesses for Sale" in local publications or websites.

Posting your own "Wanted to Buy" ad describing what you are looking for is another option. It's also advantageous to talk to the chamber of commerce in areas/regions in which you may be interested in purchasing a business.

Remember, just because a business isn't listed doesn't mean it isn't for sale. Talk to business owners in the industry; many of them might not have their companies up for sale but would consider selling if you made them an offer. Put your networking abilities and business contacts to use, and you're likely to hear of other ventures that might be good prospects. Also keep in mind that business owners who may not have thought about selling their ventures might entertain a good offer—if not immediately—over time, so follow up with anyone who wasn't adamant about not wanting to sell.

Contacting a business broker is another way to find businesses for sale. Most brokers are hired by sellers to find buyers and help negotiate deals. If you hire a broker, they will charge you a commission—typically 10 percent of the purchase price (very few may charge less). The assistance brokers can offer, especially for first-time buyers, is often worth the cost. However, if you are really trying to save money, consider hiring a broker only when you are near the final negotiating phase, at which point you might be able to broker a five percent commission. Brokers can help in several ways:

- *Prescreening businesses for you.* Good brokers turn down many of the businesses they are asked to sell, either because the seller won't provide full financial disclosure or because the business is overpriced. Going through a broker helps you avoid these bad risks.

- *Helping you pinpoint your interests.* A good broker starts by finding out about your skills and interests, then helps you select the right business for you. With the help of a broker, you may discover that an industry you had never considered is the ideal one for you.

- *Negotiating.* During the negotiating process is when brokers really earn their keep. They help both parties stay focused on the goal and smooth over problems.

- *Assisting with paperwork.* Brokers know the latest laws and regulations affecting everything from licenses and permits to financing and escrow. They also know the most efficient ways to cut through red tape, which can slash months off the purchase process. Working with a broker reduces the risk that you'll neglect some crucial form, fee, or step in the process.

A Closer Look

Whether you use a broker or go it alone, you will want to put together an *acquisition team*—your banker, accountant, and attorney—to help you. These advisors are essential to what is called *due diligence*, which means reviewing and verifying all the relevant information about the business you are considering. When due diligence is done, you will know just what you are buying and from whom.

The preliminary analysis starts with some basic questions:

- Why is this business for sale?
- What is the general perception of the industry?
- What is the general perception of this particular business?
- What is the outlook for the future of this business?
- Does—or can—the business control enough market share to stay profitable?
- If there are raw materials needed, are they in abundant supply?
- How have the company's product or service lines changed over time?

You also need to assess the company's reputation and the strength of its business relationships. Talk to existing customers, suppliers, and vendors about their relationships with the business. Scour social media accounts and reviews on sites like Google Reviews, Yelp, and elsewhere. Look for commentary on the business—and its competitors—to get a true sense of how customers view the business and whether they feel satisfied with a competitor. Contact the Better Business Bureau, industry associations, the local chamber of commerce, and licensing and credit-reporting agencies to make sure there are no complaints against the business.

Don't try to shortcut or rush this evaluation. If the business still looks promising after your preliminary analysis, your acquisition team should start examining the potential returns from the business in relation to the asking price. Whatever method you use to determine the fair market price of the business, your assessment of the value should consider such issues as the financial health, earnings history, growth potential, and intangible assets (for example, brand name and market position).

To get an idea of the company's anticipated returns and future financial needs, ask the business owner and/or accountant to show you projected financial statements. Balance sheets, income statements, cash-flow statements, footnotes, and tax returns for the past three years are all key indicators of the health of the business. These documents will help you do some financial analysis that will spotlight any underlying problems and provide a closer look at a wide range of less tangible information.

TIP

Study the financial records provided by the current business owner, but don't rely on them exclusively. Insist on seeing the tax returns for at least the past three years. Also, where applicable, ask for sales records.

Among other issues, you should focus on the following:

- *Excessive or insufficient inventory.* If the business is based on a product rather than a service, take careful stock of its inventory. First-time business buyers are often seduced by inventory, but it can be a trap. Excessive inventory may be obsolete or become so in the near future. It also costs money to store and insure. Excess inventory can mean there are a lot of dissatisfied customers who are experiencing lags between their orders and final delivery or are returning items they aren't happy with. It can also mean there has been a change in the competitive landscape, in which the market is buying newer versions of the products or different products in their place. For example, the beverage that the business sells may not be in step with the vast array of popular "healthier" beverages. Pay close attention to the market before you take over large amounts of inventory.

- *The lowest level of inventory the business can carry.* Determine this, then have the seller agree to reduce stock to that level by the date you take over the company. Also add a clause to the purchase agreement specifying that you are buying only the inventory that is current and salable.

- *Accounts receivable.* Uncollected receivables stunt the growth of a business and could require unanticipated bank loans. Look carefully at indicators such as accounts receivable turnover, credit policies, cash collection schedules, and the aging of receivables.

- *Net income.* Use a series of net income ratios to gain a better look at the bottom line of a business. For instance, the ratio of gross profit to net sales can be used to determine whether the company's profit margin is in line with that of similar businesses. Likewise, the ratio of net income to net worth, when considered together with projected increases in interest costs, total purchase price, and similar factors, can show whether you would earn a reasonable return.

Let's Make a Deal

Short on cash? Try these alternatives for financing your purchase of an existing business:

- **Use the seller's assets.** As soon as you buy the business, you'll own the assets—so why not use them to get financing now? Make a list of all the assets you're buying (along with any attached liabilities) and use it to approach banks, finance companies, and factors (companies that buy your accounts receivable).

- **Bank on purchase orders.** Factors, finance companies, and banks will lend money on receivables. Finance companies and banks will lend money on inventory. Equipment can also be sold, then leased back from equipment leasing companies.
- **Ask the seller for financing.** Motivated sellers will often provide more lenient terms and a less rigorous credit review than a bank. And unlike a conventional lender, they may take only the assets of the business as collateral. Seller financing is also flexible: the parties involved can structure the deal however they want, negotiating a payback schedule and other terms to meet their needs.
- **Use an employee stock ownership plan (ESOP).** In a larger business with a number of employees who plan to stick around, ESOPs offer you a way to get capital immediately by selling stock in the business to employees. By offering to set up an ESOP plan, you may be able to lower the sales price.
- **Lease with an option to buy.** Some sellers will let you lease a business with an option to buy. You make a down payment, become a minority stockholder, and operate the business as if it were your own.
- **Assume liabilities or decline receivables.** Reduce the sales price by either assuming the business's liabilities or having the seller keep the receivables.

Before you decide, carefully discuss any of these options with your accountant and attorney.

Finally, the ratio of net income to total assets is a strong indicator of whether the company is getting a favorable rate of return on assets. Your accountant can help you assess all these ratios. As they do so, be sure to determine whether the profit figures have been disclosed before or after taxes, and the amount of returns the current owner is getting from the business. Also assess how much of the expenses would stay the same, increase, or decrease under your management. For instance, you may decide you need to pay people more competitively to limit turnover among the best employees, thus increasing personnel expenses. But you might also recognize you can operate without rehiring a few positions and secure a more competitively priced health insurance plan than the one the current owner has in place, thus offsetting or even reducing expenses.

- *Working capital.* Working capital is defined as current assets minus current liabilities. Without sufficient working capital, a business can't stay afloat, so one key computation is the ratio of net sales to net working capital. This measures how efficiently the working capital is being used to achieve business objectives.
- *Sales activity.* Sales figures may appear rosier than they really are. When studying the rate of growth in sales and earnings, read between the lines to tell if the growth rate is due to increased sales volume or higher prices. Also examine the overall marketplace. If the market seems to be mature, sales may be static, and that might be why the seller is trying to unload the company.
- *Fixed assets.* If your analysis suggests the business has invested too much money in fixed assets, such as the plant property and equipment, make sure you know why. Unused equipment could indicate that demand is declining or that the business owner miscalculated manufacturing requirements.
- *Operating environment.* Take the time to understand the operating environment and corporate culture of the business. If the company depends on overseas clients or suppliers, for example, examine the short- and long-term political environment of the countries involved. Look at the business in light of consumer or economic trends; for example, if you are considering a store that sells products

based on a fad like Crocs, will that client base still be intact five or 10 years later? Or if the company relies on a few major clients, can you be sure they will stay with you after the deal is closed?

WARNING

Who are the employees? Beware if it's a family-run operation: Salaries may be unrealistically low, resulting in a bottom line that's unrealistically high. Or the employees you inherit may be used to a certain type of family member treatment, which means you could face pushback or end up needing to hire new employees if the family employees quit.

Law and Order

While you and your accountant review key financial ratios and performance figures, you and your attorney should investigate the legal status of the business. Look for liens against the property, pending lawsuits, guarantees, labor disputes, potential zoning changes, new proposed construction (or demolition) in the area, proposed industry regulations or restrictions, and new or pending patents; all these factors can seriously affect your business. Be sure to:

- Conduct a uniform commercial code search to uncover any recorded liens (start with city hall and check with the department of public records).
- Ask the attorneys for the business to provide a legal history of the company, and read all old and new contracts.
- Review related pending state and federal legislation, local zoning regulations, and patent histories.

Legal liabilities in business take many forms and may be hidden so deeply that even the seller honestly doesn't know they exist. How do you protect yourself? First, have your lawyer add a "hold harmless and indemnify" clause to the contract. This assures you're protected from the consequences of the seller's previous actions as owner.

TIP
Make sure you're in love with the profit potential, not just the product. Many people get emotional about buying a business, which clouds their judgment. It's important to be objective. It's also important that as much as you may love a product, you need to know (through your own research) that there is still a solid market for it.

Second, make sure your deal allows you to take over the seller's existing insurance policies on an interim basis. This gives you time to review your insurance needs at greater leisure while still making sure you have basic coverage from the minute you take over. The cost of having a lawyer evaluate a business depends on your relationship with the lawyer, the complexity of the business, and the stage at which the lawyer gets involved. Generally, costs range from $3,000 to as much as $35,000 for a comprehensive appraisal.

If you're considering buying a business that has valuable intellectual property, such as a patent, trade secret, or brand name, you may want an intellectual property attorney to evaluate it. Generally, this will cost from 0.5 to 3 percent of the business's total selling cost. Keep in mind that the average hourly rate range of an intellectual property attorney is between $275 and $380 per hour. This will be lower in some parts of the country, higher in others. You can try to secure a project-based fee, something more and more attorneys agree to these days.

Navigating Negotiations

If your financial and legal assessments show that the business is a good buy, don't be the first person to bring up the subject of price. Let the seller name the figure first, then proceed from there.

Deciding on a price, however, is just the first step in negotiating the sale. More important is how the deal is structured. You should be ready to pay at least 20 percent of the price in cash and expect to finance the remaining amount.

You can finance through a traditional lender, or sellers may agree to "hold a note," which means they accept payments over a period, just as a lender would. Many sellers like this method because it assures them of future income. Other sellers may agree to different terms—for example, accepting benefits, such as a company car for a period after the deal is completed. These methods can cut down the amount of up-front cash you need; however, you should always have an attorney review any arrangements for legality and liability issues.

TIP

Remember, you have the option to walk away from a negotiation at any point in the process if you don't like the way things are going. If you don't like the deal, don't buy. Just because you spent several months looking at a business doesn't mean you have to buy it. You have no obligation.

An individual purchasing a business has two options for structuring the deal (assuming the transaction is not a merger). The first is asset acquisition, in which you purchase only those assets you want. On the plus side, asset acquisition protects you from unwanted legal liabilities because instead of buying the corporation (and all its legal risks), you are buying only its assets.

On the downside, an asset acquisition can be expensive. The asset-by-asset purchasing process is complicated and opens the possibility that the seller may raise the price of desirable assets to offset losses from undesirable ones.

The other option is stock acquisition, in which you purchase stock. Among other things, this means you must be willing to purchase all the business's assets—and assume all its liabilities.

The final purchase contract should be structured with the help of your acquisition team to precisely reflect your understanding and intentions regarding the purchase from a financial, tax, and legal standpoint. The contract must be all-inclusive and should allow you to rescind the deal if at any time you find that the owner intentionally misrepresented the company or failed to report essential information. It's also a good idea to include a noncompete clause in the contract to ensure the seller doesn't open a competing operation down the street.

"You don't have to be a genius or a visionary or even a college graduate to be successful. You just need a framework and a dream."
—Michael Dell, founder of Dell Technologies

Transition Time

The transition to new ownership is a big change for employees of a small business. You'll need to discuss with the current owner when they want to inform the current employees of the sale. If you do this too early, they might start looking for other jobs and/or slack off, sending the business into a spiral. Conversely, you don't want to spring a major transition on people at the last minute. You'll need to work out a smooth transition with the owner and be introduced to the employees at an opportune time.

Most sellers will help you in a transition period during which they train you in operating the business. This period can range from a few weeks to several months. After the one-on-one training period, many sellers will agree to be available for phone consultation for another period. Make sure you and the seller agree on how this training will be handled, and write it into your contract. If it is too soon to tell employees about the change, you may need to do some training off premises or after business hours.

Customer Matters

During the negotiations you should discuss getting permission from the sellers to talk with their key customers. These people often have interesting insights into the business, and they can give you a better understanding of how customers feel about the business and what they would like to see changed or improved. Let them know a little about your plans and ideas for the future of the business. Getting these key people involved and excited makes the transition much easier.

If talking to key customers is a sensitive matter, you might suggest to the seller that you will tell the customers that you are a consultant, not a potential buyer.

If you buy the business lock, stock, and barrel, simply putting your name on the door and running it as before, your transition is likely to be fairly smooth. On the other hand, if you buy only part of the business's assets, such as its client list or employees, and then make a lot of changes, you'll probably face a more difficult transition.

Many new business owners have unrealistically high expectations that they can immediately make a business more profitable. Of course, you need a positive attitude to run a successful business, but if your attitude is "I'm better than you," or "I have all the answers," you'll soon face resentment from the employees, and potentially a lot of turnover.

Instead, look at the employees as valuable assets. Initially, they'll know far more about the business than you will; use that knowledge to get yourself up to speed, and treat them with respect and appreciation. Employees will inevitably feel worried about job security when a new owner takes over. That uncertainty is multiplied if you don't tell them what your plans are. Many new bosses are so eager to start running the show, they slash staff, change prices, or make other radical changes without warning employees. Involve the staff in your planning, and keep communication open so they know what is happening at all times. Ask for input, because the people who work in a company know the nuances that you have yet to learn.

Transparency is also important in such a business transaction. Taking on an existing business isn't easy, but with a little patience, honesty, and hard work, you'll soon be running things like a pro.

TIP

For more information about investigating a franchise or business opportunity, check out this helpful resource: The Federal Trade Commission (FTC) provides a free package of information about the FTC Franchise and Business Opportunity Rules that require sellers to give prospective buyers specific information to help them evaluate a business opportunity, thus ensuring that the prospective purchasers have the information they need to assess the risks of buying a work-at-home program or any other business opportunity. Visit ftc.gov.

Buying a Franchise

If buying an existing business doesn't sound right for you but starting from scratch sounds a bit intimidating, you could be suited for franchise ownership. A franchise company, as defined by Investopedia, is a business wherein the owner licenses its operations along with its products, branding, and knowledge in exchange for a franchise fee. The franchisor is the business that grants the licenses to franchisees.

"Franchising is a more symbiotic relationship where you give an opportunity to other entrepreneurs, and they run with it fueled by their own passion."
—Daymond John, Shark Tank investor, and founder and
CEO of FUBU Inc.

Essentially, the franchisee (which could be you) pays an initial fee and ongoing royalties to a franchisor. In return, the franchisee gains the use of a trademark, ongoing support from the franchisor, and the right to use the franchisor's system of doing business and selling its products or services.

McDonald's, perhaps the most well-known franchise company in the world, illustrates the benefits of franchising: Customers know they will get the same type of food, prepared the same way, whether they visit a McDonald's in Moscow or Minneapolis. Customers feel confident in McDonald's, and as a result, a new McDonald's location has a head start on success compared to an independent hamburger restaurant. In addition to a well-known brand name, buying a franchise offers many other advantages that are not available to the entrepreneur starting a business from scratch. Perhaps the most significant is that you get a proven system of operation and training. New franchisees can avoid a lot of the mistakes startup entrepreneurs typically make because the franchisor has already perfected daily operations through trial and error.

WARNING
Is a franchise or business opportunity seller doing the hustle? Watch out for a salesperson who says things like "Territories are going fast," "Act now or you'll be shut out," or "I'm leaving town on Monday, so make your decision now." Legitimate sellers will not pressure you to rush into such a big decision. If someone gives you the hustle, give that opportunity the thumbs-down.

Reputable franchisors conduct market research before selling a new outlet, so you can feel greater confidence that there is a demand for the product or service. Failing to do adequate market research is one of the biggest mistakes independent entrepreneurs make; as a franchisee, it's done for you. The franchisor also provides you with a clear picture of the competition and how to differentiate yourself from them.

Finally, franchisees enjoy the benefit of strength in numbers. You gain from economies of scale in buying materials, supplies, and services, such as advertising, as well as in negotiating for locations and lease terms. By comparison, independent operators have to negotiate on their own, usually getting less favorable terms. Some suppliers won't deal with new businesses or will reject your business because your account isn't big enough.

Top 20 Franchises

For over 40 years, *Entrepreneur* magazine has listed their Franchise 500, or the 500 most successful franchises of the year. The 2023 list features these top 20 companies:

1. Taco Bell
2. Popeyes Louisiana Kitchen
3. Jersey Mike's Subs
4. The UPS Store
5. Dunkin'
6. Kumon (Education Centers)
7. Ace Hardware
8. Culver's
9. Hampton by Hilton
10. Wingstop
11. Tropical Smoothie Cafe
12. Arby's
13. KFC Chicken
14. McDonald's

15. Wendy's
16. Servpro
17. Smoothie King
18. 7-Eleven
19. Budget Blinds
20. Snap-on Tools

Is Franchising Right for You?

An oft-quoted saying about franchising is that it puts you in business "for yourself but not by yourself." While that support can be helpful, for some entrepreneurs, it can be too restricting. Most franchisors impose strict rules on franchisees, specifying everything from how you should greet customers to how to prepare the product or service.

That's not to say you will be a mindless drone—many franchisors welcome franchisees' ideas and suggestions on how to improve the way business is done—but, for the most part, you will need to adhere to the basic systems and rules set by the franchisor. If you are fiercely independent, hate interference, and want to design every aspect of your new business, you may be better off starting your own company or buying a business opportunity.

How Much?

Franchise costs vary significantly. For example, the total investment necessary to begin operation of a traditional McDonald's franchise ranges from over $1 million to more than $2.3 million (according to McDonald's franchise information). This includes an initial franchise fee of $45,000 that must be paid to the franchisor. There will be a minimum amount for a down payment, but that varies depending on the restaurant.

> On the flip side, the website Small Business Trends lists franchises for under $10,000 in 2023, including Social Owl, Cruise Planners, Baby Boot Camp, Coffee News, BuildingStars, MobileStamp, Jazzercise, Octoclean, SiteSwan Website Builder, and Fit4Mom.
>
> You will also find many franchises with costs in between.

More and more former executives are buying franchises these days. For many of them, a franchise is an excellent way to make the transition to business ownership. As an executive, you were probably used to delegating tasks like ordering supplies, answering phones, and other administrative tasks. The transition to being an entrepreneur and doing everything for yourself can be jarring. Buying a franchise could offer the support you need in making the switch to entrepreneurship.

Franchisees are often individuals who have the wealth to buy a business but are not the creative type. Rather, they are entrepreneurial at heart and excel at management and "running the show," so to speak.

TIP

Call the appropriate agencies to see how franchising is regulated in your state. Then keep the addresses and phone numbers for key state officials on file so you can contact them later if you have specific questions.

Do Your Homework

Once you've decided a franchise is the right route for you, how do you choose the right one? With so many franchise systems to choose from, the options can be dizzying. Start by investigating various industries that interest you to find those with growth potential. Narrow the choices down to a few industries you are most interested in, then analyze your geographic area to see if there is a market for that type of business. If so, contact all the franchise companies in those fields and ask them for information. Any reputable franchise company will be happy to send you information at no cost.

Of course, don't rely solely on these promotional materials to make your decision. You also need to do your own detective work. Start by going online to look up all the magazine and newspaper articles you can find about the companies you are considering, as well as checking out Entrepreneur.com's franchise listings as noted above (entrepreneur.com/franchise). Is the company depicted favorably? Does it seem to be well managed and growing? Is it on the upswing, or are the numbers of locations dropping off?

Check with the consumer or franchise regulators in your state to see if there are any serious problems with the company you are considering. If the company or its principals have been involved in lawsuits or bankruptcies, try to determine the nature of the lawsuits: Did they involve fraud or violations of FTC regulatory laws? To find out, call the court that handled the case and request a copy of the petition or judgment.

If you live in one of the 13 states that regulate the sale of franchises (California, Hawaii, Illinois, Indiana, Maryland, Michigan, Minnesota, New York, North Dakota, Rhode Island, Virginia, Washington, and Wisconsin), contact the state franchise authority, which can tell you if the company has complied with state registration. You can also visit FranchiseSolutions.com for a map of franchise registration and franchise filing status. If the company is registered with Dun & Bradstreet (D&B), request a D&B report, which will give you details on the company's financial standing, payment promptness, and other information. And, of course, it never hurts to check with your local office of the Better Business Bureau for complaints against the company.

Does the company still sound good? That means your investigation is just beginning. If you have not already received one, contact the franchisor again and ask for a copy of its Franchise

Disclosure Document or FDD (previously known as a Uniform Franchise Offering Circular, or UFOC). This disclosure document must, by law, be given to all prospective franchisees 10 business days before any agreement is signed. If changes are made to the FDD, an additional five days are added to the 10-day "cooling off" period. If a company says it is a franchise but will not give you an FDD, then contact the FTC—and take your business elsewhere.

WARNING
Exaggerated profit claims are common in franchise and business opportunity sales. Is a company promising you will make $10,000 a month in your spare time? If it is a franchise, any statement about earnings (regarding others in the system or your potential earnings) must appear in the FDD. Read the FDD and talk to five franchise owners who have attained the earnings claimed.

The FDD is a treasure trove of information for those who are serious about franchising. It contains an extensive written description of the company, the investment amount and fees required, any litigation and/or bankruptcy history of the franchisor and its officers, the trademark you will be licensed to use, the products you are required to purchase, the advertising program, and the contractual obligations of both franchisor and franchisee. It specifies how much working capital is required, equipment needs, and ongoing royalties. It also contains a sample copy of the franchise agreement you will be asked to sign should you buy into the system, as well as three years' worth of the franchisor's audited financial statements.

The FDD has been revamped to include less "legalese" and be more readable, so there is no excuse for failing to carefully read yours. Before you make any decisions about purchasing the franchise, your attorney and accountant should read it as well.

TIP

Don't be seduced by the glitz and glamour at trade shows. Keep your notebook with a checklist and your questions in hand to keep your eyes and mind on the same page.

Calling All Franchisees

One of the most important parts of the FDD is a listing of existing franchisees as well as franchisees who've been terminated or have chosen not to renew. Both lists will include mailing addresses (possibly email addresses as well) and phone numbers. If the list of terminated franchisees seems unusually long, it could be an indication that there's some trouble with the franchisor. Call or email the former franchisees, and ask them why the agreement was terminated, whether the franchisee wasn't making the grade, or whether they had some type of grievance with the franchisor.

Next, choose a random sample of current franchisees to interview in person. This is perhaps the most important step in your research. Don't rely on a few carefully selected names the franchisor gives you; pick your own candidates to talk to. Use social media (LinkedIn, Facebook, and so on.) to find people whose communities and prior experience are similar enough to yours to get insights that will truly be valuable to you.

Many franchisees and franchising experts say there's no better way to cap off your research than by spending time in a franchisee's location to see what your life will be like. Buyers should spend at least one week working in a unit. This is the best way for the franchisor and franchisee to evaluate each other. Offer to work for free. If the franchisor doesn't want you to, you should be skeptical about the investment.

When all your research is completed, the choice between two equally sound franchises often comes down to your gut instinct. That's why talking to franchisees and visiting locations are so important in the selection process.

WARNING

If your visits with current franchisees result in each one telling you they are unhappy or would not make the investment in this franchise again, think long and hard about your own decision. If they feel the franchisor has let them down or has a flawed program, you should look more carefully before taking the plunge.

Proven Purchase

Buying a franchise can be a good way to lessen the risk of business ownership. Some entrepreneurs cut that risk still further by purchasing an existing franchise—one that is already up and running. Not only does an existing franchise have a customer base, but it also has a management system already in place and ongoing revenues. In short, it already has a foundation—something that is very attractive to a lot of entrepreneurs.

Finding existing franchisees who are willing to sell is simply a matter of asking the parent company what's available. You can also check local classified ads, or visit Franchising.com or FranchiseOpportunities.com, which list thousands of businesses for sale. Once you have found some likely candidates, the investigation process combines the same steps used in buying an existing business with those used in buying a franchise. The good news, however, is that you'll get far more detailed financial information than you would when assessing a franchise company. Where other potential franchisees just get vague suggestions of potential earnings, you'll get hard facts.

Of course, there is a price to pay for all the advantages of buying an existing franchise: it is generally much costlier. In fact, the purchase price of an existing location can be two to four times more than what you would pay for a new franchise from the same company. Because you are investing more money, it is even more important to make sure you have audited financial statements and to review them with your CPA.

Once in a while, you'll find a franchise that isn't doing well. Perhaps the current owner isn't good at marketing, isn't putting forth enough effort, or isn't following the system correctly. In this case, you may be able to get the existing franchise for what it would cost to buy a new franchise—or even less. It's crucial, however, to make sure the problem is something you can correct and that you'll be able to get the location up to speed fast. After all, you're going to have immediate overhead expenses—for employees, royalties, and operating costs—so you need some immediate income as well.

Also be aware that even if a particular franchise location is thriving, it does not necessarily mean the parent company is equally successful. In fact, sometimes franchisees who know the parent company is in trouble will try to unload their franchises before the franchisor goes under. Carefully assess the franchisor's strength, accessibility, and the level of assistance they provide. Do not settle for anything less than you would when buying a new franchise.

TIP
Put yourself in the franchisor's shoes. You want to deliver an FDD only to qualified candidates who appear serious about the investment because each copy costs several dollars to reproduce. Show you are serious about their program and are genuinely interested in the information in the FDD, and you increase your chance of receiving one early in the process.

Buying a Business Opportunity
If a franchise sounds too restrictive for you, but the idea of coming up with your own business idea, systems, and procedures sounds intimidating, there is a middle ground: business opportunities.

A business opportunity, in the simplest terms, is a packaged business investment that allows the buyer to begin a business. (Technically, all franchises are business opportunities, but not all business opportunities are franchises.)

Unlike a franchise, the business opportunity seller typically exercises no control over the buyer's business operations. In fact, in most business opportunity programs, there is no continuing relationship between the seller and the buyer after the sale.

Although business opportunities offer less support than franchises, this could be an advantage for you if you thrive on freedom. Typically, you will not be obligated to follow the strict specifications and detailed program that franchisees must follow. With most business opportunities, you would simply buy a set of equipment or materials, then you can operate the business any way and under any name you want. There are no ongoing royalties in most cases, and no trademark rights are sold.

However, this same lack of long-term commitment is also a business opportunity's chief disadvantage. Because there is no continuing relationship, the world of business opportunities does have more than its share of con artists who promise buyers instant success, then take their money and run. While increased regulation of business opportunities has dramatically lessened the likelihood of rip-offs, it is still important to investigate an opportunity thoroughly before you invest any money.

Legal Matters

In general, a business opportunity refers to one of a number of ways to get into business. These include the following:

- Dealers/distributors are individuals or businesses that purchase the right to sell ABC Corp.'s products but not the right to use ABC's trade name. For example, an autho-rized dealer of Minolta products might have a Minolta sign in their window, but they can't call their business

Minolta. Often, the words *dealers* and *distributors* are used interchangeably, but there is a difference: a distributor may sell to several dealers, while a dealer usually sells direct to retailers or consumers.

- Licensees have the right to use the seller's trade name and certain methods, equipment, technology, or product lines. If business opportunity XYZ has a special technique for reglazing porcelain, for instance, it will teach you the method and sell you the supplies and machinery needed to open your own business. You can call your business XYZ, but you are an independent licensee.
- Vending machines are provided by the seller, who may also help you find locations for them. You restock your own machines and collect the money.
- Cooperatives allow an existing business to affiliate with a network of similar businesses, usually for advertising and promotional purposes.
- Direct sales.

You might also go to the North American Securities Administrators Association (NASAA), which represents state and provincial securities regulators in the United States, Canada, and Mexico. At NASAA.org, you can find a list of which states regulate business opportunities, and for that matter, which states regulate franchise opportunities.

And of course, before entering any packaged business opportunity, have your attorney check it out. They may be able to delve more deeply into the legitimacy of the business. Some are above board; many others are not.

On the Level?

Direct sales is a type of business opportunity that is very popular with people looking for part-time, flexible businesses. Some of the best-known companies in America, including Avon, Mary Kay Cosmetics, and Tupperware, fall under the direct-selling umbrella. More recent entrants like Stella & Dot and Rodan + Fields cater to fashion, accessories, and skin care. You or someone in your family might have been invited to a party at someone's home for one of these.

Direct-selling programs feature a low up-front investment—usually only a few hundred dollars for the purchase of a product sample kit—and the opportunity to sell a product line directly to friends, family, and other personal contacts. Most direct-selling programs also ask participants to recruit other sales representatives. These recruits constitute a rep's *downline*, and their sales generate income for those above them in the program.

Things get sticky when a direct sales network compensates participants primarily for recruiting others rather than for selling the company's products or services. Unfortunately, this is far too common in this type of "sales." A direct-selling system in which most of the revenues come from recruitment may be considered an illegal pyramid scheme. Even those who have found a way around the law are typically unethical. Because direct-selling programs are usually exempt from business opportunity regulation and are not defined as franchises under state and federal franchise laws, they can often find legal loopholes to jump through. You will need to do your own investigation before investing any money into these "businesses." What's more, many direct-selling businesses have come under fire for requiring business owners to buy monthly minimums of inventory to stay in good standing or even qualify to earn commissions—whether or not they're able to sell the merchandise.

Often, there are far more people selling the merchandise than there is a market for sales in a region. As a result, many recruited sales-people end up with 100 bottles or tubes of some so-called great new product in their homes with few potential customers. It's kind of like having 100 Girl Scouts all trying to sell cookies on the same block. And since you have no further dealings with the business owners, you're hung out to dry. Often, that's how "it works," and you're stuck with product you cannot sell.

Conduct a detailed Google search for news stories and legal issues along with customer and owner reviews and warnings. For more information, you can also check out the Direct Selling Association's website at dsa.org.

WARNING

Watch out for promises from third-party location hunters. The sales rep may say, "We'll place those pistachio dispensers in prime locations in your town," but more likely you'll find out that all the best locations are taken, and the next thing you know, your garage is filled with pistachio dispensers. The solution: get in your car, and check for available locations.

If a seller meets the definition of a business opportunity in states that regulate them, it generally means they must register the offering with the state authorities and deliver a disclosure document to prospective buyers at least 10 business days before the sale is made. For the most up-to-date information on states' regulations, check with consumer protection agencies—which are often a part of the attorney general's office—in your state.

Trust Your BBB

The Better Business Bureau is one place where you can check out direct sales opportunities.

If a direct sales business has a less-than-stellar reputation, you might see a warning posted like the one below that was received by a direct sales business.

CURRENT ALERTS FOR THIS BUSINESS
Pattern of Complaints:
BBB has received a pattern of complaints from consumers alleging that after trying to cancel with the business, they continue to receive additional products. Consumers also state that they have found additional charges being taken that the business has not informed them would be occurring. Complaints also allege that the business continues to bill after cancellation, and consumers are not informed that there is a $50 cancellation fee.

Checking It Out

Researching a business opportunity is a more challenging task than investigating a franchise opportunity. And if the business opportunity you are considering does not provide buyers with a disclosure document, you get a lot less information, so you have to do a lot more legwork on your own.

Whenever possible, follow the same steps you would for investigating a franchise.

Check to see if the company is registered with D&B. If it is, a financial report will give you details on its financial standing and other information.

Also check with the regulatory agency—either the Commission of Securities or the Commission of Financial Institutions—in the state where the business opportunity has its headquarters. This will tell you if the company is complying with all state regulations. If you discover that the company or its principals have been involved in lawsuits or bankruptcies, try to find out more details. Did the suits involve fraud or violations of regulatory laws? A copy of the petition or judgment, which you can get from the court that handled the case, will give you the answers.

Finally, see if the business opportunity seller will provide you with a list of people who have purchased the opportunity. Don't let the seller give you a few handpicked names; ask for a full list of buyers in your state. Check sites like LinkedIn and Facebook for sellers in your state or region if necessary. Try to track them down, and talk to as many as you can. Were they satisfied with the opportunity? Would they recommend it to friends?

The path to buying a business opportunity is not as clearly defined as the road leading to franchise ownership. The good news, however, is that you have more freedom to make your business opportunity work. More so than with a franchise, the success or failure of your business opportunity depends on you, your commitment to the venture, and the level of effort you put into it. Put that same effort into finding the right business opportunity program, and your chances of success increase exponentially.

WARNING
While it is fine to meet with someone outside of a business location to discuss a potential opportunity, the meeting should be conducted in a businesslike manner. If you find yourself in someone's living room, a basement, or another nonbusiness location, and the atmosphere resembles that of a rally rather than a business meeting, it's time to pack up and leave.

PART 2
Planning

CHAPTER 6
Choose Your Target

Defining Your Market

YOU'VE COME UP WITH A GREAT IDEA for a business . . . that's excellent! But you're not ready to roll yet. Before you go any further, the next crucial step is figuring out who your market is.

There are two basic markets you can sell to: consumer and business. These divisions are fairly obvious. If you are selling women's clothing from a retail store, your target market is consumers; if you are selling office supplies, your target market is businesses (this is referred to as *B2B* sales). In some cases—for example, if you run a printing business—you may be marketing to both businesses and individuals.

No business—particularly a small one—can be all things to all people. The more narrowly you can define your target market at the start, the better. This process is known as *creating a niche* and is a key to success for even the biggest companies. Walmart and Tiffany are both retailers, but they each have a defined niche. Walmart caters to bargain-minded shoppers, while Tiffany appeals to upscale jewelry consumers.

"Many people talk about 'finding' a niche as if it were something under a rock or at the end of the rainbow, ready-made. That is nonsense," says Lynda Falkenstein, author of *Nichecraft: Using Your Specialness to Focus Your Business, Corner Your Market, and Make Customers Seek You Out* (Niche PR, 2000). A good niche does not just fall into your lap; it must be very carefully crafted.

WARNING

Even though many baby boomers are now well over 55, don't make the mistake of marketing to them the same way you would to seniors. Boomers don't think of themselves as your stereotypical "seniors." The moral? The same marketing approaches that appealed to boomers when they were 30 will appeal to them when they're 50, 60, and 70.

Direct Hit

Once upon a time, business owners thought it was enough to market their products or services to 18-to-49-year-olds. Those days are a thing of the past. The consumer marketplace has become so differentiated, it's a misconception to talk about the marketplace in any kind of general, grand way. You can market to socioeconomic status, gender, region, lifestyle, technological sophistication, or any of numerous niche markets. You can market to Millennials, a generation that shops and buys goods and services in vastly different ways than their older siblings and parents. You can market to online-first consumers, to those who spend most of their free time on social media—and so much more. There's no end to the number of different ways you can slice the pie.

Further complicating matters, age no longer means what it used to. Fifty-five-year-old baby boomers prefer rock 'n' roll to supper clubs; some 30-year-olds may still be living with their parents. People now repeat stages and recycle their lives. Generational marketing, which defines consumers not just by age, but also by social, economic, demographic, and psychological factors, has been used since the early 1980s to give a more accurate picture of the target consumer. It's still valuable, but it can't be the only measure you employ.

Consider the value of cohort marketing, which studies groups of people who underwent the same experiences during their formative years. This leads them to form a bond and behave differently from people in different cohorts, even when they are similar in age. For instance, people who were young adults during the Great Depression behave differently from people who came of age during World War II even though they are close in age. And more recently, those who were young adults amid the Great Recession view their purchases differently than those who entered adulthood amid the dotcom bust, even though there are only five to seven years between the age groups.

To get an even narrower reading, some entrepreneurs combine cohort or generational marketing with life stages, or what people are doing at various times in their lives (going to college, getting married, having children, or retiring), and physiographic, or physical conditions related to age (nearsightedness, arthritis, or menopause).

Today's consumers are more marketing-savvy than ever and don't like to be lumped with others, so be sure you understand your niche. While pinpointing your market so narrowly takes a little extra effort, entrepreneurs who aim at a smaller target are far more likely to make a direct hit. Various finely tuned marketing tools and even easy-to-use social media ad targeting can make this easier.

There is, however, the point at which your niche can be so narrow that the market is simply too small. A women's shoe store selling only brown sandals or an ice cream parlor that serves only vanilla might be just a tad too narrow. The point is, you want to find a large enough niche that you can cover and turn a profit while trying not to spread yourself too thin. You also want a niche that has lasting power. If your niche is based on a passing fad, you may not last long.

That's important because rather than creating a niche, many entrepreneurs make the mistake of falling into the "all over the map" trap, claiming they can do many things and be good at all of them. These people quickly learn a tough lesson, Falkenstein warns: "Smaller is bigger in business, and smaller is not all over the map; it's highly focused." This doesn't mean your products can't be found all over the world; it means that they will be appreciated by customers whose wants and needs meet your niche.

Crafting Your Niche

Keep It Fresh

Once your niche is established and well received by your market, you may be tempted to rest on your laurels. This is not a good idea, says Falkenstein. "[You must] keep growing by re-niching. This doesn't mean totally changing your focus but further adapting it to the environment around you."

Ask yourself the following questions when you think you have found your niche, then put it into your calendar as a reminder to ask them again every six months or so to make sure your niche is still on target:

- Who are your target clients?
- Who aren't your target clients?
- Is your niche in a constant state of evolution?
- Does your niche offer what prospective customers want?
- Do you have a plan and delivery system that effectively conveys the need for your niche to the right market?
- Can you confidently predict the life cycle of your niche?
- How can your niche be expanded into a variety of products or services that act as profit centers?
- Do you have a sense of passion and focused energy with respect to your niche?
- Does your niche feel comfortable and natural?
- Is your niche meeting your goals in the short term?
- Does your niche have lasting power?

Hot Niche Markets to Tap Into

While there are numerous niche categories to choose from, it's always advantageous to look at what some of the hottest or growing niches are when you're starting out. If some of the popular niches interest you, then it's time to zero in and do your research. You can find a more specific market within the niche. For example, pet products are a booming business, yet you can narrow that to food toys, only cat or dog products, and so forth. Remember, the key to a successful niche is being narrow enough to attract your specific audience but not so narrow that you won't have enough choices to keep them coming back.

Among the growing areas of interest you may find your niche in include:

- Eco-friendly products
- Baby clothes
- Bathroom accessories
- Preplanned meals and home food delivery
- Weight-loss products
- Smartphone accessories
- Cannabis and CBD products
- Drones
- Health care, skin care, and beauty products
- Viral personal coaching

These are just a few popular niche categories you could investigate if they interest you. There are many others. Do your research and discover what interests you and has a big enough market to make your business profitable.

On a Mission

Once you have designed a niche for your business, you're ready to create a mission statement. A key tool that can be as important as your business plan, a mission statement captures, in a few succinct sentences, the essence of your business goals and the philosophies underlying them. Equally important, the mission statement signals what your business is all about to your customers, employees, suppliers, and the community.

The mission statement reflects every facet of your business: the range and nature of the products you offer, pricing, quality, service, marketplace position, growth potential, use of technology, and your relationships with your customers, employees, suppliers, competitors, and the community.

"Mission statements help clarify what business you are in, your goals, and your objectives," says Rhonda Abrams, author of *Successful Business Plan: Secrets & Strategies* (Planning Shop, 2014).

Your mission statement should reflect your business's specific niche. Studying mission statements from other companies can fuel your creativity. Here is a sample mission statement Abrams developed:

> AAA Inc. is a spunky, imaginative food products and service company aimed at offering high-quality, moderately priced, occasionally unusual foods using only natural ingredients. We view ourselves as partners with our customers, our employees, our community, and our environment. We aim to become a regionally recognized brand name, capitalizing on the sustained interest in Southwestern and Mexican food. Our goal is moderate growth, annual profitability, and maintaining our sense of humor.

Or consider the statement one entrepreneur developed for her consulting business: "ABC Enterprises is a company devoted to developing human potential. Our mission is to help people create innovative solutions and make informed choices to improve their lives. We motivate and encourage others to achieve personal and professional fulfillment. Our motto is: Together, we believe that the best in each of us enriches all of us."

Or consider this statement from Betterment, a financial technology firm aimed at Millennial investors: "You deserve a better way to invest. We have one mission: To empower you to make the most of your money, so you can live better."

TIP

When it comes to mission statements, employees are number one. It's more important to communicate your mission statement to employees than to your customers. The most effective mission statements are developed first for internal communication and discussion. In other words, your mission statement doesn't have to be clever or catchy marketing speak—just accurate and something you will truly live by.

CHAPTER 7

If You Build It, Will They Come?

Conducting Market Research

SO YOU HAVE A GREAT IDEA FOR A PRODUCT—something that's bound to capture the hearts and minds (and wallets) of consumers everywhere. Or perhaps you have stumbled on a service that is greatly needed today. This is your opportunity! Don't hesitate ... don't look back ... jump right into it and ...

Wait! Before you shift into high gear, you must determine whether there really is a market for your product or service. Not only that, but you need to ascertain what—if any—fine-tuning is needed. Quite simply, you must conduct market research.

Many business owners neglect this crucial step in product development for the sole reason that they don't want to hear any negative feedback. They are convinced their product or service is perfect just the way it is, and they don't want to risk tampering with it.

Other entrepreneurs bypass market research because they fear it will be too expensive. With all the other startup costs you're facing, it's not easy to justify spending money on research that will only prove what you knew all along: your product, or service, is a winner. But what if it's not?

Regardless of the reason, failing to do market research can amount to a death sentence for your business. Therefore, you must consider market research to be an important investment in your future. If you make the necessary adjustments to your product or service now, you'll save money in the long run.

"There's only one boss—the customer."
—Sam Walton, founder of Walmart

What It Is, What It Does

What exactly is market research? Simply put, market research gives you data on your customers so you can develop a marketing plan that works for your business. It enables you to identify the specific segments within a market that you want to target and to create an identity for your products or services that separates you from your competitors. Market research can also help you choose the best way to reach your customers and even the best geographic or virtual location in which to launch your new business.

TIP

When doing any type of survey, whether it is a focus group, a questionnaire, or an online survey, pay attention to customers who complain or give you negative feedback. You don't need to worry about the customers who love your product or service. It's the ones who tell you where you're going wrong who provide valuable information to help you improve.

Before you start your market research, it's a good idea to read up on market research on the internet, take an online course, meet with a marketing consultant, or even talk to a business or marketing professor at a local college or university. These sources can offer guidance and help you with the first step in market research: deciding exactly what information you need to gather.

As a rule of thumb, market research should provide you with

information about three critical areas: the industry, the consumer, and the competition.

1. *Industry information.* In researching the industry, look for the latest trends. Review the statistics and look for growth in the industry. What areas of the industry appear to be expanding, and what areas are declining? Is the industry catering to new types of customers? What technological developments are affecting the industry? How can you use them to your advantage? A thriving, stable industry is key; you don't want to start a new business in a field that is on the decline.

2. *Consumer close-up.* On the consumer side, you want to do market research. First, you want to look for the demographics in your industry, and you can find a lot of basics online. You want to get a clear picture of your customers.

   Then, once you have studied the potential customer base, get an idea of their purchasing power based on the area's per capita income, median income level, the unemployment rate, population, and other demographic factors. Determine the current sales volume in the area for the type of product or service you want to sell.

   Finally, estimate how much of the total sales volume you can reasonably obtain. (This last step is extremely important. Opening your new business in a given community won't necessarily generate additional business volume; it may simply redistribute the business that's already there.)

3. *Competition close-up.* Based on a combination of industry research and consumer research, a clearer picture of your competition will emerge. Do not underestimate the number of competitors. Keep an eye out for potential future competitors as well as current ones.

4. Examine the number of competitors on a local and, if relevant, national scale. Study their strategies and operations.

Your analysis should supply a clear picture of potential threats, opportunities, and the weaknesses and strengths of the competition facing your new business.

When looking at the competition, try to see what trends have been established in the industry and whether there is an opportunity or advantage for your business. Use the internet and other secondary research sources described later in this chapter to research competitors. Read as many articles as you can on the companies you will be competing with. If you are researching publicly owned companies, contact them and obtain copies of their annual reports. These often show not only how successful a company is but also what products or services it plans to emphasize (or de-emphasize) in the future.

Know Thy Enemy

You may recall the saying "keep your friends close and your enemies closer." Not that your competition has to be your enemy, but it's good to keep a close eye on what they are doing.

There are two ways to define competitors. One is by strategic groups—competitors who use similar marketing strategies, sell similar products, or have similar skills. Under this definition, you might group Toyota and Nissan as competitors within the car industry.

The second way to group competitors is by customer—how strongly do they compete for the same customer dollars? Using this method gives you a closer view of your competitors and the challenges they could pose to your new business.

Suppose you're thinking of opening a family entertainment center. If there are no other family entertainment centers in the area, you might think you have no competitors. Wrong! Any type of business that competes for customers' leisure time and entertainment dollars is a competitor. That means children's play centers, amusement parks, and arcades are all your competitors. So are businesses that, on the surface, don't appear similar, such as stores that sell video games. You could even face competition from nonprofit entities like public parks and beaches. In short, anything that families might do in their leisure time is your "competition." And let's not forget the lure of Netflix, online gaming, and all sorts of electronic entertainment options at home.

What do you do? Play detective. Put yourself in your competitors' shoes and analyze their strategies. As mentioned earlier, visit their stores. Talk to their customers (subtly, of course) and find out what they like and dislike about your competitors. Remember, whatever your competitors don't provide in products and services that their customers want is exactly what you should provide.

Use the internet to dig up as much information as you can about them. Find out what their tactics and goals are, and what their clients and employees have to say about them. Also, read reviews from customers and even check out employee comments on Glassdoor.com.

One of the best websites for researching the competition is D&B Hoovers (www.dnb.com), which, for a fee, provides in-depth profiles of more than 265 million companies. However, there is also free content available, and you can sign up for a free trial subscription.

When it comes to local competitors, you can visit them in person. However, if you're running a business online, you'll obviously want to visit their websites, which you can also do for national companies. When visiting competitors, you can simply browse as if you were a customer and ask some basic questions.

Market Research Methods

When you conduct your market research, you will gather two types of data: primary and secondary. Primary research is information that comes directly from the source—that is, potential customers. You can compile this information yourself (as noted above) and/or hire someone else to gather it for you via surveys, focus groups, and other methods. Secondary research involves gathering statistics, reports, studies, and other data from organizations such as government agencies, trade associations, your local chamber of commerce, and local websites.

Secondary Research

Most of your research is often secondary research. While large companies spend huge amounts of money on market research, the good news is that plenty of information is available for free to entrepreneurs on a tight budget. The best place to start? The internet.

Two good sources to look for: ThomasNet (www.thomasnet.com), an online resource that connects industrial buyers and sellers, as well as D&B Hoovers, mentioned earlier. Both sources can be found at most libraries and can help you target businesses in a particular industry, read up on competitors, or find manufacturers for your product.

To get insights into consumer markets, check out the Statistical Abstract of the United States, a statistical portrait of social, political, demographic, and economic conditions in America. The Statistical Abstract was published by the U.S. Census Bureau, starting in 1878, through 2011 (when they terminated the project). In 2012 Rowman & Littlefield and ProQuest took over the publication of this comprehensive statistical portrait of America. You can find the book at most libraries. (The latest edition as of this writing is 2022). It contains a wealth of social, political, and economic data. Ask reference librarians for other resources targeted at your specific business as well.

FYI

In the business of ecommerce? Comscore (www.comscore.com) is a market research company that will evaluate your ecommerce site.

They offer a variety of options, from web-based marketing strategies to custom research. Even if you're not ready for professional advice, exploring the site will give you an idea of the questions you should be asking in your own research. You can also find insights (for a fee in some cases) on ecommerce marketing at IBISWorld (www.ibisworld.com) and NPD Group (www.npdgroup.com), among others.

Associations

Your industry trade association can offer a wealth of information, such as market statistics, lists of members, and books and reference materials. Talking to others in your association can be one of the most valuable ways of gaining informal data about a region or customer base.

Visit the Directory of Associations at directoryofassociations.com or look in the *Encyclopedia of Associations* (Gale Cengage Learning), found in most libraries, to find associations relevant to your industry. You may also want to investigate your customers' trade associations for information that can help you market to them. Most trade associations provide information free of charge.

Read your trade associations' publications and visit their websites, as well as those aimed at your target customers, to get an idea of current and future trends and buying patterns. And keep an eye out for more: New websites, industry magazines, and newsletters are launched every year. If you're not following all of them, you could be missing out on valuable information about new products and your competitors.

On the Internet

Most market research today is done on the internet. You can Google whatever companies you are looking for and find a host of information on the leading players in your town, city, region, or in other parts of the country or the world. You can get a slew of articles, blogs, statistics, and other data on trends, demographics for various products and services, and so much more. One great place to start your market research is on Feedspot's listing of the "Top Market Research Websites, Blogs & Influencers." This is updated often and can be found at blog.feedspot.com/market_ research_blogs/.

Here you can find and read blogs from Nielsen, Forrester, GreenBook, the GlobalWebIndex, Global Market Insights, and 70 more from around the nation and around the globe.

You'll also find links to hundreds of online market research resources at KnowThis.com. Simply type in what you want to do—and you'll get results for a myriad of resources.

FYI

SurveyMonkey.com makes market research easy. You can create surveys online using a variety of templates. And if you don't know who to send your survey to, you can "buy responses" with SurveyMonkey Audience. Another option is to post your survey on your website or in a social media group (the most effective sites are Facebook and LinkedIn). SurveyMonkey will even calculate the results for you.

MarketResearch.com is a source for research reports from more than 720 publishers consolidated into one accessible collection that's updated daily. No subscription fee is required, and with its slice-and-dice Profound feature (Profound.com), you pay only for the parts of the report you need. After paying, the information is delivered to your personal library on the site.

Don't forget the terrific job the U.S. Census Bureau does at gathering data. Go to data.census.gov/cedsci/ to get census information, including a "Maps" feature.

If you don't have time to investigate online services yourself, consider hiring some industrious students to gather data from the web. Give them the parameters of what you're looking for, pay a fair rate, and let them loose on the internet, where most students are quite at home.

Government Guidance

Government agencies are an invaluable source of market research, most of it free. Almost every county government publishes population density and distribution figures in widely available census tracts. These publications will show you the number of people living in specific areas, such as precincts, water districts, or even 10-block neighborhoods. Some counties publish reports on population trends that show the population 10 years ago, five years ago, and today. Watch out for a static, declining, or small population; ideally, you want to locate where there is an expanding population that wants your products and services.

Check local employment figures for the area too. A stagnant job market—or worse, a consistently declining one—could mean that fewer people will be able to spend money, even on necessities. But it could also mean that a product or service that is less expensive than what's available might be in demand.

In addition to the sites listed above, the U.S. Census Bureau also offers a more detailed look into the intersection of business trends and population, most of which is available on the internet:

- The Census Bureau's *State and Metropolitan Area Data Book* offers statistics for metropolitan areas, central cities, and counties.
- *County Business Patterns* is an excellent Census product that reports the number of a given type of business in a county by zip code and metropolitan and micropolitan statistical areas.
- The *Economic Census* is published every five years and provides breakdowns by geographic area.

Most of these products should be available online or at your local library. If not, contact your nearest Census office for a list of publications and ordering information, log on to census.gov/library/publications.html, or call (800) 923-8282.

"You must be the change you wish to see in the world."
—Mahatma Gandhi

The U.S. government has an official web portal that is another good source of information. At USA.gov you'll find a one-stop link to all the information and services the federal government provides for the business community. Want information on benefits, grants, loans, jobs, unemployment, and taxes for small businesses? You may be able to find your answers at usa.gov/business.

Or you might try the Commerce Department's Economic Indicators web page at commerce.gov/. Literally every day, they're releasing key economic indicators from the Bureau of Economic Analysis and the U.S. Census Bureau.

If you're planning to get into exporting, contact the Department of Commerce's International Trade Administration (ITA) at trade.gov. The ITA publishes several thousand reports and statistical surveys, not to mention hundreds of books on everything American entrepreneurs need to know about exporting. Many of the reports and books are available for downloading immediately from the ITA's press and publications department (trade.gov/publications). There you'll also find information on how to order printed copies, including archived publications. Or if you prefer, call the Trade Information Center at (800) USA-TRADE.

Of course, at some point you'll need to find out about taxes. It's not fun, but it's important to get your tax questions answered by the IRS (irs.gov) and by your accountant, which we'll discuss later.

Maps

Maps of trading areas in counties and states are available from chambers of commerce, trade development commissions, industrial development boards, and local newspaper offices. These maps show the major areas of commerce and can help you judge the accessibility of various sites. Access is an important consideration in determining the limits of your market area. For more about mapping, visit MappingAnalytics.com, where you can check out their custom mapping services (look under "Map Creation").

Survey Says . . .

"A recent survey shows . . ." just might be the most overused, misused, and abused phrase in modern life. Try hard enough, and you can find a survey to prove that four out of five Americans have been aboard a UFO or are convinced that unicorns exist and there is at least one at the nearest zoo. With all the half-baked surveys out there, how do you know what to believe?

First, consider the source. Many surveys are conducted by trade associations, which inevitably are biased in favor of good news. This doesn't mean trade association surveys are necessarily inaccurate; just keep in mind that they are likely to play up positive results and downplay negative ones. When looking at any survey, consider what the source has to gain from the information presented. Then you'll have a better idea of whether to take the information seriously or with a grain of salt.

What's more, these days you need to consider how the survey is conducted—no matter the source. Social media surveys and online polls aren't going to be as scientific and might not be reliable. However, carefully targeted surveys given to targeted groups can yield valuable insight—it's still qualitative, not quantitative.

Meaningful surveys generally share the following characteristics:

- **Short-term focus.** In general, respondents are more likely to be accurate when they make predictions about the next three to six months. When it comes to predicting the long term (a year or more ahead), they're usually guessing.
- **Adequate sample size.** What constitutes adequate size depends on the topic you're surveying. In general, the broader the topic, the larger the number of respondents should be. If the survey talks about broad manufacturing trends, for example, it should survey 1,000 companies or more. Also consider where the respondents come from. If you're starting a small regional business, a large national sample may not be relevant to your needs because the sample size from your area is probably too small to tell you anything about your region.
- **Knowledgeable respondents.** Asking entrepreneurs in the electronics business to forecast the future of the industry obviously carries more weight than asking the same question of teachers or random people on the street. On the flip side, however, if you're trying to get a feel for how user-friendly your technology is for end users, you might get an unrealistic response by polling too many tech experts. People who are *too* knowledgeable on a topic may skew your survey results. Look for a diverse sampling for the best results.
- **Continual replication.** The best surveys are repeated regularly, using the same methods, so there is a good basis for comparison from survey to survey.
- **Specific information relevant to your business.** In a nutshell, the best surveys are those where respondents answer questions that are narrowly targeted to your region and niche.
- **Respondent friendly.** The most effective surveys are easy to read and understand. The more ambiguous or vague the questions are, the less likely you are to get good results.
- **Bias free.** If your survey shows bias, your results will be skewed. If, for example, you phrase certain answers in a more positive or negative light, you can get the answers you'd like to see rather than unbiased results.

Colleges and Universities

Local colleges and universities are valuable sources of information. Many college business departments have students who are eager to work in the "real world," gathering information and doing research at little or no cost.

Local business schools are a great source of experts. Many business professors do consulting on the side, and some will even be happy to offer you marketing, sales, strategic planning, or financial information for free. Call or email professors who specialize in these areas; if they can't help, they'll be able to put you in touch with someone who can. Oftentimes, their entrepreneurship students will be required to do practical work for their courses—they are often eager to connect with local small business owners (or those about to launch) to do hands-on projects and research under the watchful eye of their professors. And it's free!

College websites often have a great deal of data gathered in their archives. You may need to pay to search, but it can be worthwhile.

Community Organizations

Your local chamber of commerce or business development agency can supply useful information. They are usually free of charge, including assistance with site selection, demographic reports, and directories of local businesses. They may also offer seminars on marketing and related topics that can help you do better research.

D&B

Financial and business services firm Dun & Bradstreet (D&B), mentioned earlier, offers a range of reference sources that can help startups. Some of the information they offer as part of their Sales & Marketing Solutions are directories for career opportunities, consultants, service companies, and regional businesses. Visit their website at www.dnb.com, or call (844) 604-2173 for more information. Check out these products:

- *D&B's Regional Business Directories* provide detailed information to help identify new business prospects and assess market potential. Besides basic information (telephone number, address, and company description), the directories also tell when the company was started, sales volume, number of employees, parent company (if any), and if it's a public company, on which exchange it's traded.
- *D&B's Million Dollar Database* can help you develop a marketing campaign for B2B sales. The Million Dollar Database lists more than 34 million companies. It has complete information on U.S. and Canadian leading public and private companies and includes information regarding the number of employees, annual sales, and ownership type. The database includes information on companies in over 200 countries worldwide as well as biographical information on owners and officers, giving insight into their backgrounds and business experience. You will need to register for the Million Dollar Database. For more information, search for D&B Million Dollar Database or try https://forbeslibrary.org/databases/db-million-dollar-database/.

Primary Research

The secondary research you conduct should help you focus your niche and get a better idea of the challenges facing your business. To get a complete picture of your target market, however, you'll need to do some primary research as well.

A market research firm can help you if you feel that primary research is too complicated or time-consuming for you to do on your own. These firms will charge a few thousand dollars or more, but depending on the complexity of the information you need, you may feel this is money well spent. Your local chamber of commerce can recommend firms or individuals who can conduct market research for smaller businesses on a budget.

If you need assistance but don't want to spend that kind of cash, you can go to your SBA district office for guidance, and counselors can help you figure out what types of questions you need to ask your target market. As with secondary research, the SBA, Small Business Development Centers, colleges, and universities are good sources of help with primary research.

"The time when you need to do something is when no one else is willing to do it, when people are saying it can't be done."
—Mary Frances Berry, Geraldine R. Segal Professor of American Social Thought at the University of Pennsylvania

Group Questions and Answers

Whether you use students, get help from the SBA, use a market research firm, or go it alone, there are simple ways you can get primary research information:

- *Focus groups.* A focus group consists of five to 12 potential customers who are asked their opinions in a group interview. Participants should fit your target market—for example, single men ages 18 to 25 or working mothers. To find participants, just go to your local mall or college campus, and ask people fitting your customer profile if they would answer a few questions. Interview potential participants to get an idea of who they are and what they do. You may want to weed out people who know the ins and outs of your industry or those who you don't think will take the survey honestly. You should expect to pay between $75 and $125 per participant in focus groups. Although focus group interviews are informal, you should have a list of questions to help you direct the discussion. Start by asking whether your product or service is one the participants would buy. If so, what is the highest price they would pay? Where would they shop for such a product? Do they like or dislike the product's packaging? Your questions should center on predetermined objectives, such as determining how high you can price your product or service or what to name your business.

If you're going the do-it-yourself route, you will probably act as the focus group moderator. Encourage an open-ended flow of conversation; be sure to solicit comments from quieter members, or you may end up getting all your information from only the talkative participants. Be prepared in advance and practice with some friends. It looks easy to moderate, but you have to be ready to ask and answer questions while remaining unbiased. Not so easy when there are clearly answers you want to hear. This is why unbiased moderators are often selected to run the show.

TIP

Small fries have big ideas that could help your business grow. If you are starting a child-related business, consider using children as marketing consultants. Kids think creatively—a big asset for entrepreneurs trying to reach this market. Companies like Microsoft and those who bring you the numerous computer games that occupy too much of your kid's time often hire kids to learn their views. But you don't need to be so formal: Just try polling the kids you know. Get their responses, and ask them for suggestions.

- *Email interviews.* Give clear instructions on how to respond, and be appreciative in advance for the data you get back. Remember, keep it simple and concise—nobody wants to spend 10 minutes trying to figure out a question, nor do they want to take a survey that seems endless. Two hundred questions won't fly.

- *Social interviews.* Similar to surveys and email interviews, reaching out to groups on social media (consider Facebook, LinkedIn, and some niche social media sites) that fit into your target profile can give you a ready—and engaged—group of respondents to question.
- *Google it.* Google Surveys is a newer tool that the search giant offers for a reasonable cost. The survey costs are based on price per completed response. For a single question to the general population, it's $0.10 per completed question. Then the price ranges from $1.10 to $3.50 per completed question for two to 10 questions at a time. Google targets the specific audience you're looking for with customized survey questions (typically 10 or less) and tallies the data. You aren't charged for incomplete surveys, but you receive the data from partially completed surveys (along with fully completed ones) nonetheless. The surveys can run until you've received the level of credible insights you need.
- *Don't forget SurveyMonkey* (surveymonkey.com).

TIP

People are more likely to respond to surveys if you give them something. It should be simple and cost-effective. Perhaps it's a free download or a 10 percent discount on something you sell. A small something can serve as incentive for the few minutes it will take them to fill out your survey.

Direct Mail, Email, and Online Surveys

Direct mail has almost gone the way of the Dodo bird—it's rare. Email has changed the landscape because it's easier and quicker to send an email and less expensive to reach out to many people. Sure, people can delete an email just like they can toss your direct mail piece in the garbage. The difference is you're not losing money from the many people who will hit "delete."

When sending email surveys, you need to get recipients' permission, which means you need their email. Your website is a great place to capture email addresses. If you offer a free download, small discount, or something inexpensive in exchange for their email address and answering a short survey, that's a great way to attract visitors to your site. And short online surveys or opinion polls are a simple way to ask broad questions.

Regardless of how you design your surveys, the concept is similar: you're trying to reach out to a large audience whom you don't know, with questions that can benefit you and your business strategies. If you do use actual direct mail, you have the advantage of providing a rare piece of snail mail that won't have much competition when it's time to be opened and read. You are, however, still spending far more time and money to get a list and mail them out, plus it's a slow process.

Simple Surveys

Make your survey easy for respondents to answer. For example, instead of having lines for them to write in answers, you can give them three or four choices or offer a 1-to-4 type of response, from 1 "don't care for it" to 4 "loved it!"

People respond best to things that are not overly complicated. Also, do not ask for a lot of extraneous information from participants. You want their names, email addresses, and phone numbers. You don't need things like mother's maiden name or favorite flavor of lollipop (unless you sell lollipops). Keep it simple.

CHAPTER 8
Make It Legal

Choosing a Business Structure

OF ALL THE DECISIONS YOU MAKE when starting a business, probably the most important one relating to taxes is the type of legal structure you select for your company.

Not only will this decision have an impact on how much you pay in taxes, but it will also affect the amount of paperwork your business is required to do, the personal liability you face, and your ability to raise money.

The most common forms of business are sole proprietorship, partnership, corporation, and S corporation. Many business owners also choose to form their company as a limited liability company (LLC) or a limited liability partnership (LLP). Because each business structure comes with different tax consequences, you will want to make your selection wisely and choose the structure that most closely matches your business's needs.

If you decide to start your business as a sole proprietorship but later decide to take on partners, you can reorganize as a partnership or other entity. If you do this, be sure you notify the IRS as well as your state tax agency.

TIP

Small business owners can benefit from structuring as an LLC but being taxed as an S corporation. This gives you the tax planning options of an S corporation while having fewer of the administrative duties that come from being an LLC.

Sole Proprietorship

The simplest structure is the sole proprietorship, which usually involves just one individual who owns and operates the enterprise. If you intend to work alone, this structure may be the way to go.

The tax aspects of a sole proprietorship are appealing because the expenses and your income from the business are included on your personal income tax return, Form 1040. Your profits and losses are recorded on a form called Schedule C, which is filed with your 1040. The "bottom-line amount" from Schedule C is then transferred to your personal tax return. This is especially attractive because business losses you suffer may offset the income you have earned from your other sources.

Beginning in 2018, sole proprietors are entitled to take a deduction of 20 percent of their qualified business income earned from the business. Qualified business income is generally thought of as the company's ordinary, noninvestment income—that is, the revenue the business exists to generate minus allowable expenses. The new deduction is limited to the lesser of the 20 percent of qualified income or 50 percent of the W-2 wages paid by the business. Regardless, this new deduction puts sole proprietors (as well as S corporations and some partnerships) on a footing much more like any other giant corporation. Currently, this provision ends after the 2025 tax year.

As a sole proprietor, you must also file a Schedule SE with Form 1040. You use Schedule SE to calculate how much self-employment tax you owe. In addition to paying annual self-employment taxes, you must make estimated tax payments if you expect to owe at least $1,000 in federal taxes for the year after deducting your withholding and credits, and your withholding will be less than the smaller of: (1) 90 percent of the tax to be shown on your current year tax return or (2) 100 percent of your previous year's tax liability. The federal government permits you to pay estimated taxes in four equal amounts throughout the year on the 15th of April, June, September, and January. With a sole proprietorship, your business earnings are taxed only once, unlike other business structures. Another big plus is that you will have complete control over your business—you make all the decisions.

TIP
If you operate as a sole proprietor, be sure you keep your business income and records separate from your personal finances. It helps to establish a business checking account and get a credit card to use only for business expenses. This will be invaluable at tax time and help you keep your accounts in order.

There are a few disadvantages to consider, however. Selecting the sole proprietorship business structure means you are personally responsible for your company's liabilities. As a result, you are placing your assets at risk, and they could be seized to satisfy a business debt or a legal claim filed against you.

Raising money for a sole proprietorship can also be difficult. Banks and other financing sources may be reluctant to make business loans to sole proprietorships. In most cases, you will have to depend on your financing sources, such as savings, home equity, or family loans.

"Success seems to be connected to action. Successful people keep moving. They make mistakes, but they never quit."
—J. Willard Marriott, founder of Marriott International Inc.

Partnership
If your business will be owned and operated by several individuals, you'll want to take a look at structuring your business as a partnership. Partnerships come in two varieties: general or limited partnerships. In a general partnership, the partners manage the company and assume responsibility for the partnership's debts

and other obligations. A limited partnership has both general and limited partners. The general partners own and operate the business and assume liability for the partnership, while the limited partners serve as investors only; they have no control over the company and are not subject to the same liabilities as the general partners.

Unless you expect to have many passive investors, limited partnerships are generally not the best choice for a new business because of all the required filings and administrative complexities. If you have two or more partners who want to be actively involved, a general partnership would be much easier to form.

One of the major advantages of a partnership is the tax treatment it enjoys. A partnership does not pay tax on its income but "passes through" any profits or losses to the individual partners. At tax time, the partnership must file a tax return (Form 1065) that reports its income and loss to the IRS. In addition, each partner reports their share of income and loss on Schedule K-1 of Form 1065.

Personal liability is a major concern if you use a general partnership to structure your business. Like sole proprietors, general partners are personally liable for the partnership's obligations and debts. Each general partner can act on behalf of the partnership, take out loans, and make decisions that will affect and be binding on all the partners (if the partnership agreement permits). Keep in mind that partnerships are also more expensive to establish than sole proprietorships because they require more legal and accounting services.

Howdy, Partner!

If you decide to organize your business as a partnership, be sure you draft a partnership agreement that details how business decisions are made, how disputes are resolved, and how to handle a buyout. You'll be glad you have this agreement if for some reason you run into difficulties with one of the partners or if someone wants out of the arrangement.

The agreement should address the purpose of the business and the authority and responsibility of each partner. It's a good idea to consult an attorney experienced with small businesses for help in drafting the agreement. Here are some other issues you'll want the agreement to address:

- **How will the ownership interest be shared?** It's not necessary, for example, for two owners to equally share ownership and authority. However, if you decide to do it, make sure the proportion is stated clearly in the agreement. In many cases owners are not equal partners, which is fine, as long as it is spelled out in the agreement.

- **How will responsibilities be divided?** Who oversees marketing? Who will be in charge of hiring and HR issues? Who will head up accounting and finances? Purchasing? Production? Inventory? IT? Companies will differ in their needs, but one partner will have to take responsibility for each department.

- **How will decisions be made?** It's a good idea to establish voting rights in case a major disagreement arises. When just two partners own the business 50-50, there's the possibility of a deadlock. To avoid a deadlock, some businesses provide in advance for a third partner, a trusted associate who may own only two percent of the business—so you remain equal partners at 49-49—but whose vote can break a tie.

- **When one partner withdraws, how will the purchase price be determined?** One possibility is to agree on a neutral third party, such as your banker or accountant, to find an appraiser to determine the price of the partnership interest. A forensic accountant is another possible third party to consider.

- **If a partner withdraws from the partnership, when will the money be paid?** Depending on the partnership agreement, you can agree that the money will be paid over three, five, or 10 years, possibly with interest. You don't want to be hit with a cash-flow crisis if the entire price has to be paid on the spot in one lump sum.

Corporation

A corporation is an independent legal entity, separate from its owners, and as such, it requires complying with more regulations and tax requirements. But tax legislation passed at the end of 2017 gives corporations certain benefits in the years 2018 through 2025 that might be worth that hassle.

The biggest benefit for a business owner who decides to incorporate is the liability protection they receive. A corporation's debt is not considered that of its owners, so if you organize your business as a corporation, you are not putting your personal assets at risk. A corporation can also retain some of its profits without the owner paying tax on them.

Another plus is the ability of a corporation to raise money. A corporation can sell stock, either common or preferred, to raise funds. Corporations also continue indefinitely, even if one of the shareholders dies, sells the shares, or becomes disabled. The corporate structure, however, comes with several downsides. A major one is higher costs.

Corporations are formed under the laws of each state with its own set of regulations. You will probably need the assistance of an attorney to guide you. In addition, because a corporation must follow more complex rules and regulations than a partnership or sole proprietorship, it requires more accounting and tax preparation services.

WARNING

Many cities require even the smallest enterprises to have a business license. Municipalities are mainly concerned with whether the area where the business is operating is zoned for its intended purpose and whether there's adequate customer parking available. You may even need a zoning variance to operate in some cities. According to Bizfluent.com, the average business license in the United States costs roughly $75 to $100.

The ABCs of LLCs

Limited liability companies (LLCs) have been around since 1977, but their popularity among entrepreneurs has solidified in the last decade or two. An LLC is a hybrid entity, bringing together some of the best features of partnerships and corporations. The advantage of an LLC over a sole proprietorship is that the owner is not personally responsible for the liabilities of the company if appropriate business formalities are followed.

Like a sole proprietorship, earnings flow to the owner, are taxed only at the personal level, and are subject to the self-employment tax. LLCs can elect to be taxed as a sole proprietor (one owner), partnership (more than one owner), or corporation. While somewhat more complex than a sole proprietorship, establishing an LLC is relatively simple. There is no limitation on the number of shareholders an LLC can have. In addition, any member or owner of the LLC is allowed a full participatory role in the business's operation; in a limited partnership, on the other hand, the limited partners are not permitted any say in the operation. However, one thing to note about LLCs, explains tax and legal expert Mark J. Kohler, is that for many small businesses—even sole proprietors with no employees—an S corporation may offer more tax advantages once your business generates as little as $30,000 to $40,000 annually. An LLC can elect to be taxed as a sole proprietor, partnership, or corporation. So, the 20 percent deduction would apply to an LLC that elects pass-through taxation.

Another drawback to forming a corporation: owners of the corporation pay a double tax on the business's earnings. Not only are corporations subject to corporate income tax at both the federal and state levels, but any earnings distributed to shareholders in the form of dividends are taxed at individual tax rates on their personal income tax returns. This burden has been lightened for S corps with a 20 percent pass-through allowance passed as part of the tax reform package approved by Congress at the end of 2017.

One strategy to help soften the blow of double taxation is to pay some money out as salary to yourself and perhaps to other corporate shareholders who work for the company. A corporation is currently not required to pay tax on earnings paid as reasonable compensation, and it can deduct the payments as a business expense. However, the IRS has limits on what it believes to be reasonable compensation. Again, check these limits for changes over time.

WARNING
Any money you've invested in a corporation is at risk. Despite the liability protection of a corporation, most banks and many suppliers require business owners to sign a personal guarantee so they know corporate owners will make good on any debt if the corporation can't.

S Corporation

The S corporation is more attractive to small business owners than a regular (or C) corporation. That's because an S corporation has some appealing tax benefits and still provides business owners with the liability protection of a corporation. With an S corporation, income and losses are passed through to shareholders and included on their individual tax returns. As a result, there's just one level of federal tax to pay. And for many S corporations, that level of taxes was reduced with the tax legislation package passed in late 2017. For tax years 2018 through 2025, the legislation allows S corporations to take a 20 percent deduction on business income.

In addition, owners of S corporations who don't have inventory can use the cash method of accounting, which is simpler than the accrual method. Under this method, income is taxable when received and expenses are deductible when paid.

S corporations can also have up to 100 shareholders. This makes it possible to have more investors and thus attract more capital, tax experts maintain.

S corporations do come with some downsides. For example, S corporations are subject to many of the same rules corporations must follow, and that means higher legal and tax service costs. They also must file articles of incorporation, hold directors' and share-holders' meetings, keep corporate minutes, and allow shareholders to vote on major corporate decisions. The legal and accounting costs of setting up an S corporation are also similar to those for a regular corporation.

WARNING
Like an LLC, the owner of an S corporation is not personally responsible for the liabilities of the company. However, one note of caution is that if the formalities of setting up and running an S corporation are not followed, the owner's protection from the liabilities of the company may be forfeited.

Finding Success with "S"

Under the tax legislation passed in late 2017, the advantages of an S corporation might be more evident over an LLC. If you bring in $100,000 in revenue and spend $50,000 on expenses, as an LLC, your taxes could reach the 45 percent rate, explains tax and legal expert Mark J. Kohler. But if your company is set up as an S corporation, you might take a salary of $40,000 and file a Schedule K-1 (which reports income, losses, deduc-tions, and credits), saving about $9,000 in taxes. Add to that the 20 percent deduction on the remaining $60,000 that the new tax law provides, and you'd only be paying taxes on the remaining $48,000. An LLC can elect to be taxed as a sole proprietor, partnership, or corporation. The 20 percent deduction could apply to the LLC if pass-through income is elected.

Some expenses incurred by S corporations cannot be deducted under the newer tax laws. The COVID-19 relief package passed in 2020 did put some deductions back in play for small business owners through at least 2022, including some meals (including a 100% deduction for restaurant meals), as well as some charitable giving that was previously capped. Check the IRS website at www.irs.gov for the latest information on what you can deduct.

Another major difference between a regular corporation and an S corporation is that S corporations can only issue one class of stock. Experts say this can hamper the company's ability to raise capital.

In addition, unlike in a regular corporation, S corporation stock can only be owned by individuals, estates, and certain types of trusts.

WARNING

If you anticipate several years of losses in your business, keep in mind you cannot deduct corporate losses on your personal tax return. However, business structures such as partnerships, sole proprietorships, and S corporations allow you to take those deductions. LLCs that elect pass-through taxation can also pass losses to a personal tax return.

Putting Inc. to Paper

To start the process of incorporating, contact the secretary of state or the state office that is responsible for registering corporations in your state. Ask for instructions, forms, and fee schedules on incorporating.

It is possible to file for incorporation without the help of an attorney by using books and software to guide you. Your expense will be the cost of these resources, the filing fees, and other costs associated with incorporating in your state.

If you do it yourself, you will save the expense of using a lawyer, which can cost $500 to $5,000 if you choose a firm that specializes in startup businesses. The disadvantage is that the process may take you some time to accomplish. There is also a chance you could miss some small but important detail in your state's law. You can, however, check legal websites such as LegalZoom.com and Nolo.com.

One of the first steps in the incorporation process is to prepare a certificate or articles of incorporation. Some states provide a printed form for this, which either you or your attorney can complete. The information requested includes the proposed name of the corporation, the purpose of the corporation, the names and addresses of those incorporating, and the location of the principal office of the corporation. The corporation will also need a set of bylaws that describe in greater detail than the articles how the corporation will run, including the responsibilities of the company's shareholders, directors, and officers; when stockholder meetings will be held; and other details important to running the company. Once your articles of incorporation are accepted, the secretary of state's office will send you a certificate of incorporation.

"Nobody can be a success if they don't love their work."
—David Sarnoff, Chairman of RCA

In Other Words

If you are starting a sole proprietorship or a partnership, you have the option of choosing a business name, or dba (doing business as), for your business. This is known as a fictitious business name. If you want to operate your business under a name other than your own (for instance, Carol Axelrod doing business as "Darling Donut Shoppe"), you may be required by the county, city, or state to register your fictitious name.

Procedures for doing this vary among states. In many states, all you have to do is go to the county offices and pay a registration fee to the county clerk. In other states, you also have to place a fictitious name ad in a local newspaper for a certain length of time. The cost of filing a fictitious name notice ranges from about $40 to $125. Your local bank may require a certificate to show that you are doing business as a name other than your own to open a business account for you; if so, a bank officer can tell you where to go to register.

In most states, corporations don't have to file fictitious business names unless the owner(s) do business under a name other than their own. In effect, incorporation documents are to corporate businesses what fictitious name filings are to sole proprietorships and partnerships.

Rules of the Road

Once you are incorporated, be sure to follow the rules of incorporation. If you fail to do so, a court can pierce the corporate veil and hold you and the other business owners personally liable for the business debts.

It is important to follow all the rules required by state law. You should keep accurate financial records for the corporation, showing a separation between the corporation's income and expenses and those of the owners.

The corporation should also issue stock, file annual reports, and hold yearly meetings to elect company officers and directors, even if they're the same people as the shareholders. Be sure to keep minutes of shareholders' and directors' meetings. On all references to your business, make certain to identify it as a corporation, using Inc. or Corp., whichever your state requires. You also want to make sure that whomever you will be dealing with, such as your banker or clients, knows that you are an officer of a corporation.

Setting Up an LLC

If limited liability is not a concern for your business, you could begin as a sole proprietorship or a partnership so "passed through" losses in the early years of the company can be used to offset your other income. After the business becomes profitable, you may want to consider another type of legal structure.

To set up an LLC, you must file articles of organization with the secretary of state in the state where you intend to do business. Some states also require you to file an operating agreement, which is similar to a partnership agreement. Like partnerships, LLCs do not have perpetual life. Some state statutes stipulate that the company must dissolve after 30 years. Technically, the company dissolves when a member dies, quits, or retires.

If you plan to operate in several states, you must determine how a state will treat an LLC formed in another state. If you decide on an LLC structure, be sure to use the services of an experienced accountant who is familiar with the various rules and regulations of LLCs. If you expect to have a partner in the LLC, consider the costs of establishing the LLC in each of the states you live in. For instance, it costs about one-quarter as much to establish an LLC in New York as it does in California.

Another recent development is the limited liability partnership (LLP). With an LLP, the general partners have limited liability. For example, the partners are liable for their own malpractice and not that of their partners. This legal form works well for those involved in a professional practice, such as physicians.

FYI

To help sort through the business structure maze, you can obtain free IRS publications—*Partnerships* (Publication 541), *Corporations* (Publication 542), and *Taxation of Limited Liability Companies* (Publication 3402)—by downloading them from the IRS website at www.irs.gov.

The Nonprofit Option

What about organizing your venture as a nonprofit organization? Unlike a for-profit business, a nonprofit may be eligible for certain benefits, such as sales, property, and income tax exemptions at the state level. The IRS points out that while most federal tax-exempt organizations are nonprofit organizations, organizing as a nonprofit at the state level does not automatically grant you an exemption from federal income tax.

Another major difference between a profit and nonprofit business deals with the treatment of the profits. With a for-profit business, the owners and shareholders generally receive the profits. With a nonprofit, any money that is left after the organization has paid its bills is put back into the organization. Some types of nonprofits can receive contributions that are tax deductible to the individual who contributes to the organization. Keep in mind that nonprofits are organized to provide some benefit to the public.

Nonprofits are incorporated under the laws of the state in which they are established. To receive federal tax-exempt status, the organization must apply with the IRS. First, you must have an Employer Identification Number (EIN) and then apply for recognition of exemption by filing Form 1023 (Application for Recognition of Exemption Under Section 501(c)(3) of the Internal Revenue Code) or Form 1024 (Application for Recognition of Exemption under Section 501(a)) with the necessary filing fee. Both forms are available online at www.irs.gov.

The IRS identifies the different types of nonprofit organizations by the tax code under which they qualify for exempt status. One of the most common forms is 501(c)(3), which is set up to do charitable, educational, scientific, religious, and literary work. This includes a wide range of organizations, from continuing education centers to outpatient clinics and hospitals.

The IRS also mandates that there are certain activities tax-exempt organizations cannot engage in if they want to keep their exempt status. For example, a section 501(c)(3) organization cannot intervene in political campaigns.

Remember, nonprofits still have to pay employment taxes, but in some states, they may be exempt from paying sales tax. Check with your state to make sure you understand how nonprofit status is treated in your area. In addition, nonprofits may be hit with unrelated business income tax. This is regular income from a trade or business that is not substantially related to the charitable purpose. Any exempt organization under Section 501(a) or Section 527(a) must file Form 990-T (Exempt Organization Business Income Tax Return) if it has gross income of $1,000 or more from an unrelated business and pay tax on the income.

If your nonprofit has revenues of more than $25,000 a year, be sure to file an annual report (Form 990) with the IRS. Form 990-EZ is a shortened version of 990 and is designed for use by small exempt organizations with incomes of less than $1 million.

Form 990 asks you to provide information on the organization's income, expenses, and staff salaries. You also may have to comply with a similar state requirement. The IRS report must be made available for public review. If you use the calendar year as your accounting period, file Form 990 by May 15.

For more information on IRS tax-exempt status, download IRS Publication 557, *Tax-Exempt Status for Your Organization* at www.irs.gov.

Even after you settle on a business structure, remember that the circumstances that make one type of business organization favorable are always subject to changes in the laws. It makes sense to reassess your form of business from time to time to make sure you are using the one that provides the most benefits.

"To be successful in business, you need friends. To be very successful, you need enemies."
—Christopher Ondaatje, Canadian Financier and Philanthropist

CHAPTER 9
Plan of Attack

Creating a Winning Business Plan

SOME PEOPLE THINK YOU DON'T NEED A BUSINESS PLAN unless you're trying to borrow money. Of course, it's true that you do need a good plan if you intend to approach a lender—whether a banker, a venture capitalist, or any number of other sources—for startup capital. But a business plan can be more than a pitch for financing; it can serve as a guide to help you define and meet your business goals.

Do I Really Need a Business Plan?

For many entrepreneurs, the answer is going to be yes. But for many people, a formal, full-on business plan is only necessary if you are going to be looking for money—be it a loan, an investment, or a partner who will contribute financially to the company. But according to some experts, outside those reasons, you don't need a detailed, formal plan.

Marketing and research consultant Gene Marks explains in his *Fortune* magazine column "Practically Speaking," "Most of my clients that run established companies don't do it. But here's something you should do: Have an informal plan. Create a spreadsheet of quarterly objectives, both quantitative (sales and margin goals, cash-flow expectations, number of orders shipped, number of quotes issued) and qualitative (a new safety program in place, a new hire completed, an upgrade to your website). This way, you can refer to your objectives, with your key people, and keep a good eye on whether you're on track. It doesn't have to be pretty, so it's not a formalized business plan that consultants like to see. But for your internal purposes, it will cut to the chase and be effective."

While there are various theories on business plans, they can generally serve as a guide.

"My interest is in the future because I am going to spend the rest of my life there."
—Charles F. Kettering, American Inventor and Scientist

What Is a Business Plan and How Do You Put One Together?

Simply stated, a business plan conveys your business goals and the strategies you'll use to meet them, potential problems that may confront your business and ways to solve them, the organizational structure of your business (including titles and responsibilities), and the amount of capital required to finance your venture and keep it going until it breaks even. A business plan won't automatically make you a success, but it will help you avoid some common causes of business failure, such as undercapitalization or lack of an adequate market.

As you research and prepare your business plan, you'll find weak spots in your business idea that you'll be able to repair. You'll also discover areas with potential you may not have thought about before—and ways to profit from them. Only by putting together a business plan can you decide whether your great idea is worth your time and investment.

Sound impressive? It can be, if put together properly. A good business plan follows generally accepted guidelines for both form and content. There are three primary parts of a business plan.

1.   The first is the *business concept*, where you discuss the industry, your business structure, your product or service, and how you plan to make your business a success.

2. The second is the *marketplace* section, in which you describe and analyze potential customers: who and where they are, what makes them buy, and so on. Here, you also describe the competition and how you will position yourself to beat it.

3. Finally, the *financial* section contains your income and cash-flow statements, balance sheet, and other financial ratios, such as break-even analyses. This part may require help from your accountant and a good spreadsheet software program.

Breaking these three major sections down further, a business plan consists of seven major components:

1. Executive summary
2. Business description
3. Market strategies
4. Competitive analysis
5. Design and development plan
6. Operations and management plan and your team
7. Financial factors

In addition to these sections, a business plan should also have a cover, title page, and table of contents.

Executive Summary

Anyone looking at your business plan will first want to know what kind of business you are starting. So, the business concept section should start with an executive summary, which outlines and describes the product or service you will sell.

The executive summary is the first thing the reader sees. Therefore, it must make an immediate impact by clearly stating the nature of the business, the customers you seek, how you solve their problems/issues, why these products/services are important, and if you are seeking capital, the type of financing you want. The executive summary describes the business, its legal form of operation (sole proprietorship, partnership, corporation, or limited liability company), the amount and purpose of the loan requested, the repayment schedule (not in great detail), the borrower's equity share, and the debt-to-equity ratio after the loan, security, or collateral is offered. Also listed are the market value, estimated value, or price quotes for any equipment you plan to purchase with the loan proceeds.

Your executive summary should be short and businesslike—generally between half a page and one page. If the use of funding or other areas will be more difficult, you can explain that they will be detailed later.

This page should generate interest and excitement about your upcoming business and your products or services.

TIP

Although it's the first part of the plan to be read, the executive summary is most effective if it's the last part you write. By waiting until you have finished the rest of your business plan, you ensure you have all the relevant information in front of you. This allows you to create an executive summary that hits all the crucial points of your plan.

Sample Executive Summary

The business will provide ecology-minded consumers with an environmentally safe disposable diaper that will feature all the elements that are popular among users of disposable diapers but will include the added benefit of biodegradability. The product, which is patent pending, will target current users of disposable diapers who are deeply concerned about the environment as well as those consumers using cloth diapers and diaper services.

The product will be distributed to wholesalers who will, in turn, sell to major supermarkets, specialty stores, department stores, and major toy stores.

The company was incorporated in 1989 in the state of California under the name of Softie Baby Care. The company's CEO, president, and vice president have more than 30 years of combined experience in the diaper industry.

With projected net sales of $871 million in its third year, the business will generate pretax net profits of 8 percent. Given this return, investment in the company is very attractive. Softie Baby Care Inc. will require a total amount of $26 million over three stages to start the business.

1. The first stage requires $8 million for product and market development.
2. The second stage of financing will demand $12 million for implementation.
3. The third stage will require $6 million for working capital until break even is reached.

First-stage capital will be used to purchase needed equipment and materials to develop the product and market it initially. To obtain its capital requirements, the company is willing to relinquish 25 percent equity to first-stage investors.

The company has applied for a patent on the primary technology that the business is built around, which allows the plastic within a disposable diaper to break down upon extended exposure to sunlight. Lease agreements are also in place for a 20,000-square-foot facility in a light industrial area of Los Angeles, as well as for major equipment needed to begin production. Currently, the company has funding of $3 million from the three principals, with purchase orders for 500,000 units already in hand.

Business Description

This section expands on the executive summary, describing your business in much greater detail. It usually starts with a description of your industry. Is the business retail, wholesale, food service, manufacturing, or service-oriented? How big is the industry? Why has it become so popular? What kinds of trends are responsible for the industry's growth? Prove, with statistics and anecdotal information, how much opportunity there is in the industry.

Explain the target market for your product or service, how the product will be distributed, and the business's support systems—that is, its advertising, promotions, and customer service strategies.

Next, describe in greater detail your product or service. Discuss the product's applications and end users. Emphasize any unique features or variations that set your product or service apart from others in your industry.

If you're using your business plan for financing purposes, explain why the money you seek will make your business more profitable. Also explain how you will use the money. Will you use the money to expand, to create a new product, or to buy new equipment?

Market Strategies

Here's where you define your market—its size, structure, growth prospects, trends, and sales potential. Based on research, interviews, and sales analysis, the marketplace section should focus on your customers and your competition. How much of the market will your product or service be able to capture?

The answer is tricky because so many variables influence it. Think of it as a combination of words and numbers. Write down the who, what, when, where, and why of your customers. The answer is critical to determining how you will develop pricing strategies and distribution channels.

Be sure to document how and from what sources you compiled

your market information. Describe how your business fits into the overall market picture. Emphasize your unique selling proposition (USP)—in other words, what makes you different? Explain why your approach is ideal for your market.

Once you've clearly defined your market and established your sales goals, present the strategies you'll use to meet those goals.

- *Price.* Thoroughly explain your pricing strategy and how it will affect the success of your product or service. Describe your projected costs and then determine pricing based on the profit percentage you expect. Costs include materials, distribution, advertising, and overhead. Many experts recommend adding 25 to 50 percent to each cost estimate, especially overhead, to ensure you don't underestimate.
- *Distribution.* This includes the entire process of moving the product from the factory to the end user. The type of distribution network you choose depends on your industry and the size of the market. How much will it cost to reach your target market? Does that market consist of upscale customers who will pay extra for a premium product or service or budget-conscious consumers looking for a good deal? Study your competitors to see what channels they use. Will you use the same channels or a different method that may give you a strategic advantage? How will you plug into these channels (are there exclusives you won't be able to break or middlemen you'll need to employ)?
- *Sales.* Explain how your sales force (if you have one) will meet its goals, including elements such as pricing flexibility, sales presentations, lead generation, and compensation policies.

FYI

Looking for inspiration? Visit the SBA website (www.sba.gov) and check out writing a business plan, which offers clear, concise business plan outlines and tutorials. When you're done, if you feel like your business plan has the right stuff, consider submitting it to a business plan competition. Universities, such as Wharton and Harvard Business School, and corporations often sponsor such competitions, offering grants and other cash prizes that can really help offset your startup costs. To find a competition, Google "business plan competition" and see what turns up.

Competitive Analysis

How does your business relate to the competition? The competitive analysis section answers this question. Using what you've learned from your market research, detail the strengths and weaknesses of your competitors, the strategies that give you a distinct advantage, any barriers you can develop to prevent new competition from entering the market (think patents, trademarks, and the like), and any weaknesses in your competitors' service or product development cycle you can turn into one of your strengths.

The competitive analysis is an important part of your business plan. Often, startup entrepreneurs mistakenly believe their product or service is the first of its kind and fail to recognize that competition exists. In reality, every business has competition, whether direct or indirect. Your plan must show that you recognize this and have a strategy for dealing with the competition. This includes competition that sells products or services in a manner different from yours. For example, brick-and-mortar businesses sometimes forget that they have plenty of online competition, while web-based businesses sometimes forget that those folks looking at their website can also go down the block to a local store. The more upfront you are about the competition, the more solid your plan will appear to anyone reviewing it.

Write Your Plan in Pencil

Bob Reiss, author of *Bootstrapping 101: Tips to Build Your Business with Limited Cash and Free Outside Help* (R&R, 2009), has been involved in 16 startups and has been the subject of not one, but two Harvard Business School case studies. His recommendation: have a business plan, but write it in pencil. Why? You will likely have to change, amend, modify, scrap, or abandon your original business plan. One of the attributes of successful entrepreneurs is flexibility, Reiss says. Writing your business plan in pencil forces you to look at change as the only constant. Make change your friend, embrace it, and work it to your benefit.

Design and Development Plan

This section describes a product's design and charts its development within the context of production, marketing, and the company itself. If you have an idea but have not developed the product or service, if you plan to improve an existing product or service, or if you own an existing company and plan to introduce a new product or service, this section is extremely important. (If your product is already completely designed and developed, or, like millions of business owners, you are selling existing products purchased through vendors, you don't need to complete this section. If you are offering a service, you will need to concentrate only on the development half of the section.)

The design section should thoroughly describe the product's design and the materials used; include any diagrams if applicable. The development plan generally covers these three areas: (1) product development, (2) market development, and (3) organizational development. If you're offering a service, cover only the last two.

Create a schedule that shows how the product, marketing strategies, and organization will develop over time. The schedule should be tied to a development budget so expenses can be tracked throughout the design and development process.

Operations and Management Plan and Your Team

Here you describe how your business will function daily. This section explains logistics, such as the responsibilities of each member of the management team, the tasks assigned to each division of the company (if applicable), and the capital and expense requirements for operating the business.

Describe the managers and their qualifications, and specify what type of support staff will be needed for the business to run efficiently. It is in this section that you should also describe your team. Financial backers not only want to invest in an idea, but in the people behind that idea. Investors want to know that you, your partners, and/or team have the knowledge and experience to make the business work. Often, in fact, anyone who's asked to lend or invest money will jump to this section right after looking at the executive summary. You can say wonderful things in the business plan and have all the numbers lined up, but if lenders/investors don't believe you (and your team) can come through, they will stop reading.

You'll also want to include any potential benefits or pitfalls to the community, such as new job creation, economic growth, and possible effects on the environment from manufacturing, and how they will be handled to comply with local, state, and federal regulations.

"Ideas are a dime a dozen, but the real meat on those bones comes from trying to realize them."
—Seth Godin, Dotcom Business Executive and Author

Finding Funding

One of the primary purposes of a business plan is to help you obtain financing for your business. When writing your plan, it's important to remember who those financing sources are likely to be.

Bankers, investors, venture capitalists, and investment advisors are sophisticated in business and financial matters. How can you ensure your plan makes the right impression? Four tips are key:

1. **Avoid hype.** While many entrepreneurs tend to be gamblers who believe in relying on their gut feelings, financial types are likely to go "by the book." If your business plan praises your idea with superlatives like "one of a kind," "unique," or "unprecedented," your readers are likely to be turned off. They also won't believe you and are more likely to look skeptically at everything else in your plan. Wild, unsubstantiated promises or unfounded conclusions tell financial sources you are inexperienced, naïve, and reckless.

2. **Polish the executive summary.** Potential investors receive so many business plans, they cannot afford to spend more than a few minutes evaluating each one. If at first glance your proposal looks dull, poorly written, unfocused, vague, or confusing, investors will toss it aside without a second thought. In other words, if your executive summary doesn't grab them, you won't get a second chance. Think of it like the cover letter of your future business.

3. **Make sure your plan is complete.** Even if your executive summary sparkles, you need to make sure the rest of your plan is just as good and that all the necessary information is included. Some entrepreneurs are in such a hurry to get financing, they submit a condensed or preliminary business plan, promising to provide more information if the recipient is interested. This approach usually backfires for two reasons: First, if you don't provide information up-front, investors will assume it doesn't exist yet and that you are stalling for time. Second, even if investors are interested in your preliminary plan, their interest may cool in the time it takes you to compile the rest of the information.

-   **Be honest.** If you are lying, using unsubstantiated information, making things up as you go, or simply guessing, you can instantly lose all credibility. Also, make sure you can support anything and everything you put on paper in your business plan.

When presenting a business plan, you are starting from a position of weakness. And if potential investors find any flaws in your plan, they gain an even greater bargaining advantage. A well-written and complete plan gives you greater negotiating power and boosts your chances of getting financing on your own terms.

Financial Factors

The financial statements are the backbone of your business plan. They show how profitable your business will be in the short and long term, and should include the following:

- The *income statement* details the business's cash-generating ability. It projects such items as revenue, expenses, capital (in the form of depreciation), and cost of goods. You should generate a monthly income statement for the business's first year, quarterly statements for the second year, and annual statements for each year thereafter (usually for three, five, or 10 years, with five being the most common).

- The *cash-flow statement* details the amount of money coming into and going out of the business—monthly for the first year and quarterly for each year thereafter. The result is a profit or loss at the end of the period represented by each column. Both profits and losses carry over to the last column to show a cumulative amount. If your cash-flow statement shows you consistently operating at a loss, you will probably need additional cash to meet expenses. Most businesses have some seasonal variations in their budgets, so reexamine your cash-flow calculations if they look identical every month.

- The *balance sheet* paints a picture of the business's financial strength in terms of assets, liabilities, and equity over a set period. You should generate a balance sheet for each year profiled in the development of your business.

After these essential financial documents, include any relevant summary information that's not included elsewhere in the plan but will significantly affect the business. This could include ratios, such as return on investment, break-even point, or return on assets. Your accountant can help you decide what information is best to include.

Many people consider the financial section of a business plan the most difficult to write. If you haven't started your business yet, how do you know what your income will be? You have a few options. The first is to enlist your accountant's help. An accountant can take your raw data and organize it into categories that will satisfy all the requirements of a financial section, including monthly and yearly sales projections. Or, if you are familiar with accounting procedures, you can do it yourself with the help of a good spreadsheet program. You can also research similar businesses and talk with others who have opened businesses in your industry.

Bplans.com

For everything business plan related, you might want to visit Bplans.com. You'll find sample plans for businesses in different industries, templates, resources, free downloads, how-to videos, and plenty of articles. It's definitely worth the time to visit bplans.com before you start writing your business plan.

A Living Document

You've put a lot of time and effort into your business plan. What happens when it's finished? A good business plan should not gather dust in a drawer. Think of it as a living document and refer to it often. A well-written plan will help you define activities and responsibilities within your business, as well as identify and achieve your goals.

To ensure that your business plan continues to serve you well, make it a habit of updating yours annually. Set aside a block of time near the beginning of the calendar year, fiscal year, or whenever is convenient for you. Meet with your accountant or financial advisor, if necessary, to go over and update financial figures. Is your business heading in the right direction, or has it wandered off course?

AHA!

Still need another reason to write a business plan? Consider this: if you decide to sell your business in the future, or if you become disabled or die and someone else takes over, a business plan will help make the transition a smooth one.

Making it a practice to review your business plan annually is a great way to start the year fresh and reinvigorated. It lets you catch any problems before they become too large to solve. It also ensures that if the possibility of getting financing, participating in a joint venture, or other such occasion arises, you'll have an updated plan ready to go so you don't miss out on a good opportunity.

Reviewing your business plan and matching it up against the actual results of your business over one, two, or five years will allow you to see how much of the plan is working as anticipated and where your plans had to be readjusted. Sometimes you'll find that you've had to deviate from your initial plan because of many factors, such as a changing competitive landscape, new rules or regulations in the industry, changes in technology, or the need to bring in more personnel or change some of the team you have in place.

For a variety of reasons, entrepreneurs cannot always stick to the letter of the business plan. This is where flexibility and knowing when you need to pivot becomes vital to a business's success. You'll need to update your business plan according to changes that have come up in your business, industry, or the economy. So you'll want to check your plan and make changes as necessary. Sometimes everything is right on track—but most often things don't go 100 percent as planned—that's what's tricky about owning and running a business. That's also why business plans shouldn't be etched in stone. Things change, and your business and business plan need to change with them.

Whether you're writing it for the first time or updating it for the fifteenth, creating a good business plan doesn't mean penning a 200-page book or adding lots of fancy clip art and footnotes. It means proving to yourself and others that you understand your business and you know what's required to make it grow and prosper.

Stacking the Deck

One of the more common ways of approaching venture capitalists is by using a pitch deck. The pitch deck is a scaled-down version of your business plan for investors who have lots of money, little time, and want the concise version (that is, venture capitalists). The deck includes the high-level information from your business plan without as much detail. On average, a pitch deck includes about 20 well-designed slides that make up your presentation. Typically, you begin with an elevator pitch, which is a brief description of an idea, product, or company that clearly explains the concept in a short time, such as the length of an elevator ride, as illustrated by actress Melanie Griffith in the 1988 movie *Working Girl.*

It's in your best interest to have a business plan, presentation, and elevator pitch all carefully planned out. Hint: Don't rush the shorter presentations—often people don't realize that writing something short and to the point can be far more difficult than writing a longer presentation.

PART 3
Funding

CHAPTER 10

All in the Family

Financing Starts with Yourself and Friends and Relatives

Once you have decided on the type of venture you want to start, the next step on the road to business success is figuring out where the money will come from to fund it. Where do you start?

The best place to begin is by looking in the mirror. Self-financing is the number one form of financing used by most business startups. In addition, when you approach other financing sources such as bankers, venture capitalists, or the government, they will want to know exactly how much of your own money you are putting into the venture. After all, if you don't have enough faith in your business to risk your own money, why should anyone else risk theirs? You need to have some "skin in the game" as they say.

Do It Yourself

Begin by doing a thorough inventory of your assets. You are likely to uncover resources you didn't know you had. Assets include savings accounts, equity in real estate, vehicles, recreational equipment, and collections. You may decide to sell some assets for cash or to use them as collateral for a loan. But you've got to be ready to dig deep into your own pockets first. For this reason, many people start putting money aside for a business venture in advance.

If you have investments, you may be able to sell some to gain some funding. Low-interest-margin loans against stocks and securities can also be arranged through your brokerage accounts.

The downside here is that if the market should fall and your securities are your loan collateral, you'll get a margin call from your broker, requesting you to supply more collateral. If you can't do that within a certain time, you'll be asked to sell some of your securities to shore up the collateral. Also look at your personal line of credit. Some businesses have successfully been started on credit cards, although this is one of the most expensive and riskiest ways to finance yourself.

If you own a home, consider getting a home equity loan on the part of the mortgage that you have already paid off. The bank will either provide a lump-sum loan payment or extend a line of credit based on the equity in your home. A line of credit is often a better choice so you can tap into it when you need it rather than spending a lump sum too quickly. Depending on the value of your home, a home equity loan could become a substantial line of credit. If you have $50,000 in equity, you could possibly set up a line of credit of up to $40,000. Some credit unions and specialty lenders will offer even more. Home equity loans carry relatively low interest rates, and all interest paid on a loan of up to $100,000 is tax-deductible. But this is risky; you need to be sure you can repay the loan—you can lose your home if you do not. For this reason, many entrepreneurs do not put their homes in jeopardy.

Consider borrowing against cash-value life insurance. You can use the value built up in a cash-value life insurance policy as a ready source of cash. The interest rates are reasonable because the insurance companies always get their money back. You don't even have to make payments if you do not want to. Neither the amount you borrow nor the interest that accrues has to be repaid. The only loss is that if you die and the debt hasn't been repaid, that money is deducted from the amount your beneficiary will receive.

"If you think you can, you can. And if you think you can't, you're right."
—Mary Kay Ash, founder of Mary Kay Cosmetics

If you have a 401(k) retirement plan through your employer and are starting a part-time business while you keep your full-time job, consider borrowing against the plan. It's common for such plans to allow you to borrow up to 50 percent of your vested account balance up to a maximum of $50,000. The interest rate is usually 1% to 2% above prime with a specified repayment schedule. The downside of borrowing from your 401(k) is that if you lose your job, the loan has to be repaid in a short period of time—often 60 days (but occasionally as long as six months)—or it is taxed heavily, as if you've taken an early withdrawal from the plan. Consult the plan's documentation to see if this is an option.

Good Benefits

If you have been laid off or lost your job, another source of startup capital may be available to you. Some states have instituted self-employment programs as part of their unemployment insurance systems.

People who are receiving unemployment benefits and meet certain requirements are recruited into entrepreneurial training programs that show them how to start businesses. This gives them an opportunity to use their unemployment funds for startup while boosting their chances of success.

Contact the department in your state that handles unemployment benefits to see if such a program is available to you.

Another option is to use the funds in your individual retirement account (IRA). Under the laws governing IRAs, you can withdraw money from an IRA as long as you replace it within 60 days. This is not a loan, so you don't pay interest. It's a withdrawal that you're allowed to keep for 60 days. It's possible for a highly organized entrepreneur to juggle funds among several IRAs. But if you're one day late—for any reason—you'll be hit with a 10 percent premature-withdrawal fee, and the money you haven't returned becomes taxable.

If you have a Roth IRA, you're entitled to withdrawals tax- and penalty-free, so long as the funds were in the account for at least five years. That's because a Roth is taxed at the time you put funds into the IRA account—not when you retire and with-draw it. Consider switching your regular IRA to a Roth over a couple of years if you know you plan to finance a business this way. You'll have to pay the taxes in the year you make the conversion, but the money will then be free to withdraw when you need it without the big penalties. Make the conversions well before you need the cash.

If you are employed, another way to finance your business is by squirreling away money from your current salary until you have enough to launch the business. If you don't want to wait, consider moonlighting or cutting your full-time job back to part time. This ensures you'll have some steady funds rolling in until your business starts to soar.

WARNING

Watch out for the relative or friend who agrees to lend you money even though they can't afford to. There will always be people who want to do anything they can to help you. Some will give you funds that they really can't spare. Be cautious not to take money from people who really need to keep it.

Be careful when taking money from retirement accounts. The reality is that businesses do not always become profitable, and in some cases, it can take a while—you don't want to jeopardize money you will need for your future.

Keep this in mind: you may have more assets than you real-ize. Use as much of your own money as possible to get started; remember, the larger your own investment, the easier it will be for you to acquire capital from other sources. But remember, you can only use the money that is above what you need for your living expenses.

Friends and Family

Your own resources may not be enough to give you the capital you need. "Most businesses are started with money from four or five different sources," says Mike McKeever, author of *How to Write a Business Plan*. After self-financing, the second most popular source for startup money is composed of friends, relatives, and business associates.

"Family and friends are great sources of financing," says Tonia Papke, president and founder of MDI Consulting. "These people know you have integrity and will grant you a loan based on the strength of your character."

It makes sense. People with whom you have close relation-ships know you are reliable and competent, so there should be no problem in asking for a loan, right? Keep in mind, however, that asking for financial help isn't the same as borrowing the car. While squeezing money out of family and friends may seem an easy alternative to dealing with bankers, it can be a much more delicate situation. Papke warns that your family members or friends may think lending you money gives them license to meddle. "And if the business fails," she says, "the issue of paying the money back can be a problem, putting the whole relationship in jeopardy."

The bottom line, says McKeever, is that "whenever you put money into a relationship that involves either friendship or love, it gets very complicated." Fortunately, there are ways to work out the details and make the business relationship advantageous for all parties. If you handle the situation correctly and tactfully, you may gain more than finances for your business—you may end up strengthening the personal relationship as well. The best way to do this is to have some conversations up-front that spell everything out clearly and help both parties separate business from their personal relationship.

The Right Source

The first step in getting financing from friends or family is finding the right person to ask for money. As you search for potential lenders or investors, don't enlist people with ulterior motives. "It's not a good idea to take money from a person if it's given with emotional strings," says McKeever. "For example, avoid borrowing from relatives or friends who have the attitude of 'I'll give you the money, but I want you to pay extra attention to me.'"

TIP

A business plan sets out the expectations for the company in writing. It shows family members who are putting up the money what they can expect for their contribution. And it helps keep the entrepreneur—you— mindful of responsibilities to family members who backed you and keeps you on track to fulfill your obligations. If your master business plan seems too complex, make a shorter version with an executive summary and some of the highlights from each section, and give it to the family members you hope will invest. Be sure to be available to explain and answer questions.

Once you determine whom you'd like to borrow money from, approach the person in an informal situation at first. Let them know a little about your business and gauge their interest. If they seem interested and say they would like more informa-tion about the business, make an appointment to meet with them in a professional atmosphere. "This makes it clear that the subject of discussion will be your business and their interest in it," says McKeever. "You may secure their initial interest in a casual setting, but to go beyond that, you have to make an extra effort. You should do a formal sales presentation and make sure the person has all the facts."

A large part of informing this person is having your business plan or a concise version of your business plan (or pitch deck) available. You should bring this to your meeting. Explain your business plan, using the plan or pitch deck to support your claims. Your goal is to get the other person on your side and make them as excited as you are about the possibilities of your business.

During your meeting—and, in fact, whenever you discuss a loan—try to separate the personal from the business as much as possible. Difficult as this may sound, it's critical to the health of your relationship. "It's important to treat the lender formally, explaining your business plan in detail rather than casually passing it off with an 'if you love me, you'll give me the money' attitude," says McKeever.

Be prepared to accept rejection gracefully and be clear with the person about the separation of personal and professional in your own mind. "Don't pile on the emotional pressure—emphasize that you'd like this to be strictly a business decision for them," says McKeever. "If relatives or friends feel they can turn you down without offending you, they're more likely to invest. Give them an out."

Putting It on Paper
Now it's time to put the loan in motion. First, you must state how much money you need, what you'll use it for, and how you'll pay it back. Next, draw up the legal papers—an agreement stating that the person will indeed put money into the business.

Too frequently, business owners fail to take the time to figure out exactly what kind of paperwork should be completed when they borrow from family or friends. "Often small business owners put more thought into figuring out what type of car to buy than how to structure this type of lending arrangement," says Steven I. Levey, formerly of accounting firm GHP Investment Advisors. Unfortunately, once you've made an error in this area, it's difficult to correct it.

Your loan agreement needs to specify whether the loan is secured (that is, the lender holds title to part of your property) or unsecured, what the payments will be, when they're due, and what the interest is. If the money is in the form of an investment, you have to establish whether the business is a partnership or corporation, and what role, if any, the investor will play. To be sure you and your family and friends have a clear idea of what financial obligations are being created, you have a mutual responsibility to make sure everyone is informed about the process and decide together how best to proceed. Getting this right from the start will also help prevent misunderstandings and, potentially, legal issues down the road.

"Outline the legal responsibilities of both parties and when and how the money should be paid back," says McKeever. If your loan agreement is complex, it's a good idea to consult your accountant about the best ways to structure the loan (see the "Taxing Matters" section following).

Whichever route you take, make sure the agreement is in writing if you expect it to be binding. "Any time you take money into a business, the law is very explicit: You must have all agreements written down and documented," says McKeever. If you don't, emotional and legal difficulties could end up in court. And if the loan isn't documented, you may find yourself with no legal recourse. You may also harbor ill will toward investors with whom you are related or friends. Money can destroy the strongest relationships.

Taxing Matters

Putting the agreement on paper also protects both you and your lender come tax time. Relying on informal and verbal agreements results in tax quagmires. You should show this agreement to your accountant and/or lawyer to get their input.

If your friend or family member wants to give you a no-interest loan, make sure the loan is not more than $100,000. If you borrow more, the IRS will slap what it considers to be market-rate interest, better known as *imputed interest,* on the lender. That means that while your friend or relative may not be receiving any interest on the money you borrowed, the IRS will tax them as if they were.

No interest is imputed if the aggregate loans are less than $10,000. Between $10,000 and $100,000, the imputed amount is limited to your net investment income, such as interest, dividends, and, in some cases, capital gains. Taxable imputed interest income to you is zero as long as the borrower's net investment income for the year is no more than $1,000. To determine the interest rate on these transactions, the IRS uses what it calls the applicable federal rate, which changes monthly. Keep in mind that if you don't put all the details of the loan in writing, it will be very difficult for you to deduct the interest you pay on it. Additionally, the relative who lent the money won't be able to take a tax deduction on the loss if you find you can't repay, and the money could be considered a gift in an audit if the paperwork isn't in order.

To be safe, Tom Ochsenschlager, vice president of taxation for the American Institute of Certified Public Accountants, recommends that you make the friend or relative who is providing the money one of the business's shareholders. This effectively makes the transaction an investment in your company and makes it easier from a tax standpoint for your friend or relative to write off the transaction as an ordinary loss if the business fails. (This applies only if the total amount your company received for its stock, including the relative's investment, does not exceed $1 million.)

SAVE

You don't necessarily need a lawyer to write your loan agreement. You can find examples of loan agreements on websites such as Rocket-Lawyer.com or LegalZoom.com; just write up the same information, complete it, and sign it. If you decide to get legal advice, you can save money by drawing up the loan agreement yourself, then giving it to an attorney to redraft. You can also use an online pay-by-document service for a legal review.

If you do decide to make your friends or relatives shareholders, be careful—if you give away shares to too many of your friends and family members, you will no longer be the owner.

In addition, "if your company is wildly successful, your relative will have an equity interest in the business, and his or her original investment will be worth quite a bit more," Ochsenschlager says. In contrast, if a relative gives you a loan and your company goes under, the relative's loss would generally be considered a personal bad debt. This creates more of a tax disadvantage because personal bad debts can be claimed as capital losses only to offset capital gains. Capital losses that exceed capital gains in a year may be used to offset ordinary taxable income up to $3,000 in any one tax year. Net capital losses in excess of $3,000 can be carried forward indefinitely until the amount is exhausted. Thus, an individual making a large loan that isn't repaid may have to wait several years to realize the tax benefits from the loss.

If the loan that can't be repaid is a business loan, however, the lender receives a deduction against ordinary income and can take deductions even before the loan becomes totally worthless. (One catch: The IRS takes a very narrow view of what qualifies as a business loan. To qualify as a business loan, it must be connected to the lender's business.) This will be difficult, so consult an accountant about the best way to structure the loan for maximum tax benefits to both parties.

Making your relative a shareholder doesn't mean you'll have to put up with Mom or Pop in the business. Depending on your company's organizational structure, your friend or relative can be a silent partner if your company is set up as a partnership, or a silent shareholder if you are organized as an S corporation or limited liability company.

Keep 'Em Happy

Even with every detail documented, your responsibilities are far from over. Don't make assumptions or take people for granted just because they are friends or family members. Communication is key.

If your relative or friend is not actively involved in the business, make sure you contact them once every month or two so you can explain how the business is going. "When people invest in small businesses, it often becomes sort of their pet project," says McKeever. "It's important to take the time to keep them informed."

And, of course, there are the payments. Though friends or relatives who invest in your business understand the risks, you must never take the loan for granted. "Don't be cavalier about paying the money back," McKeever says. "That kind of attitude could ruin the relationship."

Go to the Crowd

Did you hear the story about the bakery owner who turned to strangers to get new ovens for her shop? Or perhaps you've heard talk about lending clubs? Strangers giving money outright or lending through an organized platform have become legitimate, albeit small, sources for funding. There are two ways to finance your business using the crowd:

1. **Peer-to-peer lending (P2P).** There are several places you can check out to learn about this means of borrowing money, including LendingClub (www.lendingclub.com), Zopa (www.zopa.com), and Prosper (www.prosper.com). The process is simple: You fill out a funding request, detailing how much you need and what it will be used for. Your request will be reviewed, and based on the risk and credit rating of the applicant, you will receive an interest rate. You will then receive suggested lenders and can choose one with whom you'd like to do business. These are mostly regular people looking to earn more on their savings than a typical bank savings account might offer. They choose what they'd like to fund and earn money off the interest you're charged. You are responsible for (usually monthly) loan payments of interest as well as repaying the principal.

    P2P lending can provide higher returns for investors than most other types of investments. From your standpoint as a borrower, it is easier to go through the process successfully, and the interest rates are often lower than most financial institutions. On the other hand, lenders are taking a greater risk with borrowers who have low credit ratings. Note: there are jurisdictions where peer-to-peer lending is not allowed, so make sure it's legal in your area.

2. **Crowdfunding.** Websites such as Kickstarter (www.kickstarter.com), GoFundMe (www.gofundme.com), or Indiegogo (www.indiegogo.com) serve as platforms to get funding for your ideas. That is, if strangers like what you're trying to do. It's a simple concept: An individual or group posts an idea or cause, then markets it heavily on the site. On the other side, funders (people just like you) search for new products or initiatives to support. It's not a loan or investment. People who give money to crowdfunding projects don't receive shares or interest in return, although those seeking money do provide some incentives to those donating funds. For instance, the bakery owner who raised $26,000 for a new oven offered a batch of cookies to every funder. An artist raising money for a new gallery might offer free passes to a showing or an inexpensive print of their work.

The most successful crowdfunding campaigns start with the right mentality and approach, says Slava Rubin, cofounder of Indiegogo. After posting your campaign, you can't sit and wait for funding to come in—you've got to be proactive. "Once you are done posting your campaign and launching it, you need to keep it fresh and dynamic," Rubin advises. To ensure you catch people's attention, it's important to have a great pitch. Breaking up the text with images and videos will help grab viewers' attention while telling them more about your product, Rubin advises. Another important must-do is providing updates on your page. "Don't just sit on your story—engage with the audience."

Keep in mind that in most cases the funding platform has to approve you, and the approval process can be somewhat random. In addition, on some platforms, if you are seeking $10,000 by June 30 and you receive only $4,500, you will get the $4,500. Other platforms, however, will only give you the money if you reach the entire amount. In other words, if you don't raise the $10,000, you will receive nothing and you will have wasted time putting together a presentation and promoting it. Before doing anything, carefully review how the process works.

How Much Is Enough?

Before you begin planning for the cash needs of your business, you must figure out how much money you will need to live on for the first six to 18 months of your business's operation. The best way to accomplish this is to create a budget that shows where you spent your money in the past 12 months. Make sure you look over the whole 12-month period because expenses often change a lot from month to month. When creating the schedule, be on the lookout for expenses that could be reduced or eliminated if necessary.

CHAPTER 11

Nothing Ventured, Nothing Gained

How to Find and Attract Investors

NO MATTER WHAT TYPE OF FINANCING source you approach—a bank, a venture capitalist, or your cousin Lenny—there are two basic ways to finance a business: equity financing and debt financing. In equity financing, you receive capital in exchange for part ownership of the company. In debt financing, you receive capital in the form of a loan, which must be paid back.

Equity Basics

Equity financing can come from various sources, including venture capital firms and private investors. Whichever source you choose, there are some basics you should understand before you try to get equity capital. An investor's "share in your company" comes in various forms. If your company is incorporated, the investor might bargain for shares of stock. Or an investor who wants to be involved in the management of the company could come in as a partner.

Keeping control of your company can be more difficult when you are working with outside investors who provide equity financing. Before seeking outside investment, make the most of your own resources to build the company. The more value you can add before you go to the well, the better. If all you bring to the table is a good idea and some talent, an investor may not be willing to provide a large chunk of capital without receiving a controlling share of the ownership in return. As a result, you could end up losing control of the business you started.

Don't assume the first investor to express interest in your business is a godsend. Even someone who seems to share your vision for the company may be bad news. It pays to know your investor. This means doing your due diligence. An investor who doesn't understand your business may pull the plug at the wrong time—and destroy the company.

AHA!

One entrepreneur who wanted to open a restaurant got a list of potential investors by attending all the grand openings of restaurants in the area where he wanted to locate. By asking for the names of people who invested in those restaurants, he soon had enough contact names to finance his own business.

As Not Seen on TV

By now, nearly everyone who has dreamed of becoming an entrepreneur has seen at least one episode of *Shark Tank*. Over the years, many hopeful small business owners have pitched their products and ideas to a panel of "shark" investors, led by business leader/entrepreneur Robert Herjavec and billionaire Mark Cuban. The sharks have invested in more than 225 businesses—and they've made many additional offers on deals that were never closed. Just being on the show can boost the presence of a small business.

But pitching investors in real life isn't like the prescreened and rehearsed process you see on TV. However, there are lessons you can take from the demands the sharks make of the entrepreneurs—ones that will be useful in securing investors the traditional way. Here are six big ones:

1. **The 10-second rule.** The first 10 seconds of your pitch will set the tone and the impression investors have of you and your idea. Practice, practice, practice.

2. **Be clear and concise.** People who fail to get money or attention from the sharks typically lack clarity about their ideas and real conviction that they can succeed. Project clear goals, plans, and projections, and make sure your passion comes through.

3. **Know the problem and the market.** The sharks are notorious for homing in on the problem a business is trying to solve and how big that problem is. That helps determine the likelihood of success. You don't need a product that's going to solve a worldwide problem to have a good idea. If your business solves a problem that has a significant market and you have knowledge of that market, and a means of reaching them, you can make a strong impression. Be clear when you speak to investors about this.

4. **Do the math—and do it well.** Know the costs of making your product or running your business compared to the profits. Understand and be clear about your margins. Know the overall market size and a realistic share you can capture. Know what you plan to do with an investor's money. Commit all this to memory—and be able to back it up.

5. **Be prepared to answer questions.** Review your business plan, and be prepared to answer any possible question they could ask. Whenever contestants on *Shark Tank* fumble their way through an answer, the sharks start circling, and you know that contestant is most likely heading home without an offer.

6. **Be willing to listen and learn from feedback.** On *Shark Tank*, the sharks almost always offer smart lessons, although they're often in the form of criticism or tearing apart (as sharks would) an idea they deem unworthy of an investment. If potential investors criticize or decide not to invest, listen for the advice in that criticism, and don't be afraid to ask for feedback about what would have changed their minds. Use that to improve your pitch.

How It Works

Because equity financing involves trading partial ownership inter-est for capital, the more capital a company takes in from equity investors, the more diluted the founder's control. Expect it to be between 25 and 75 percent equity in your company. The real question is: how much management are you willing to give up?

Jerry Jendusa, former co-owner of the airplane parts manu-facturer EMTEQ, now co-owner of the business coaching firm STUCK, where entrepreneurs can get "unstuck" from business problems, warns against being too generous with equity in your business. In his book *Get Unstuck*, Jendusa points out that "when you're starting out in business and want nothing more than to entice investors, it is tempting to promise people anything to get them onboard. The problem is that cash and a level of control are your two most significant assets when it comes to growing a business. If you sacrifice these two fundamentals, you'll have no business left to grow." Jendusa goes on to mention that when you're giving away 20 percent of nothing, it's pretty easy to do. But when the business reaches the $10 million mark, you're giving away $2 million—and that's a lot to be giving up for a loan that might have been $50,000.

WARNING
Do not give up more than 49 percent of your business or you can lose everything. Even if you give away small increments and you are the largest shareholder, it's not impossible for the other shareholders to join together and vote you out if they have more shares than you do (50-plus shares). Consider yourself warned.

Don't overlook the importance of voting control in the company. Investors may be willing to accept a majority of the preferred (nonvoting) stock rather than common (voting) stock.

Another possibility is to give the investor a majority of the profits by granting dividends to the preferred stockholders first. Or holders of nonvoting stock can get liquidation preference, meaning they're first in line to recover their investment if the company goes under.

Even if they're willing to accept a minority position, financiers generally insist on contract provisions that permit them to make management changes under certain conditions. These might include covenants permitting the investor to take control of the company if the corporation fails to meet a certain income level or makes changes without the investor's permission.

Investors may ask that their preferred stock be redeemable either for common stock or for cash a specified number of years later. That gives the entrepreneur a chance to buy the company back if possible, but also may allow the investor to convert to common stock and gain control of the company.

The best way to do equity investing is to limit how much any single shareholder can have and minimize how much involvement they can have. Do this in advance so everything is spelled out. All this can be designed with your attorney and your accountant. Lean toward profit incentives so you are not giving anything away until there is something to give, and you maintain most of your business.

TIP

When it comes to pitching to investors, it's not just what you say, but also how you say it. Breathe. Enunciate. Pace yourself, speaking neither too quickly nor too slowly. Nervous? Fess up—admitting your insecurity puts the listeners on your side. Finally, remember—practice makes perfect.

Venture Capital

When most people think of equity financing, they think of venture capital. Once seen as a plentiful source of financing for startup businesses, venture capital—like most types of funding—is not easy to come by. Venture capital is one of the more popular forms of equity financing used to finance high-risk, high-return businesses. The amount of equity a venture capitalist holds is a factor of the company's stage of development when the investment occurs, the perceived risk, the amount invested, and the relationship between the entrepreneur and the venture capitalist.

Venture capitalists invest in businesses of every kind. Many individual venture capitalists prefer to invest in industries that are familiar to them, and in recent years that has often been technology.

You may get lucky on websites like *Entrepreneur's* VC 100 (www.entrepreneur.com/vc100)—a directory of the top investors in early-stage startups. And luck is very helpful when pursuing venture capitalists to invest in your business. If you think we're trying to discourage you, we are. Money can be found for investing in your company, but the era of the venture capitalist happily handing out forklifts of money is over—especially for startups.

Venture capital is most likely to be given to an established company with an already proven track record. If you are a startup, your product or service must wow them, along with your team. Sometimes those who show their incredible business acumen can woo a venture capitalist into taking a chance on them. You also must be ready to play by their rules. Venture capitalists, as part of their agreement to lend you money, typically want a say in how you do business.

The Many Faces of Venture Capital

There are several types of venture capital. If you're going to pitch for some, first understand the differences—and where you are most likely to find small successes.

- Private venture capital partnerships are perhaps the largest source of risk capital. They generally look for businesses that have the capability to generate a 30 percent return on investment each year. They like to actively participate in the planning and management of the businesses they finance and have large capital bases—up to $500 million—to invest at all stages.
- Industrial venture capital pools usually focus on funding firms that have a high likelihood of success, such as high-tech enterprises or companies using state-of-the-art technology in a unique manner.
- Investment banking firms traditionally provide expansion capital by selling a company's stock to public and private equity investors. Some also have formed their own venture capital divisions to provide risk capital for expansion and early-stage financing.
- Small Business Investment Companies (SBICs) are licensed and regulated by the SBA. SBICs are private investors that receive three to four dollars in SBA-guaranteed loans for every dollar they invest. Under the law, SBICs must invest exclusively in small firms with a net worth less than $18 million and average after-tax earnings (over the past two years) of less than $6 million. They're also restricted in the amount of private equity capital for each funding. For a complete listing of active SBICs, contact the Small Business Investor Alliance, formerly the National Association of Small Business Investment Companies, at www.sbia.org.
- Specialized Small Business Investment Companies (SSBICs) are also privately capitalized investment agencies licensed and regulated by the SBA. They are designed to aid women- and minority-owned firms, as well as businesses in socially or economically disadvantaged areas, by providing equity funds from private and public capital. SSBICs are also restricted in the amount of their private funding. For information and a directory of active SSBICs, contact the National Association of Investment Companies at www.naicpe.com.

Before approaching any investor or venture capital firm, do your homework and find out if your interests match their investment preferences. The best way to contact venture capitalists is through an introduction from another business owner, banker, attorney, or other professional who knows you and the venture capitalist well enough to approach them with the proposition.

Earth Angels

The unpleasant reality is that getting financing from venture capital firms is an extreme long shot. The pleasant reality is there are plenty of other sources you can tap for equity financing—typically with far fewer strings attached than an institutional venture capital deal. One source of private capital is an investment angel.

Originally a term used to describe investors in Broadway shows, "angel" now refers to anyone who invests their money in an entrepreneurial company (unlike institutional venture capitalists who invest other people's money). Angel investing has soared in recent years as a growing number of individuals seek better returns on their money than they can get from traditional investment vehicles. Contrary to popular belief, most angels are not millionaires. Typically, they earn anywhere from $60,000 to $200,000 a year—which means there are likely to be plenty of them right in your backyard.

Where Angels Fly

Angels can be classified into two groups: affiliated and nonaffiliated. An affiliated angel is someone who has some sort of contact with you or your business but is not necessarily related to or acquainted with you. A nonaffiliated angel has no connection with either you or your business.

"It is only as we develop others that we permanently succeed."
—Harvey Samuel Firestone,
founder of The Firestone Tire and Rubber Co.

It makes sense to start your investor search by seeking an affiliated angel because they are already familiar with you or your business and have a vested interest in the relationship. Begin by jotting down names of people who might fit the category of affiliated angel:

- *Professionals.* These include professional providers of services you now use—doctors, dentists, lawyers, accountants, and so on. You know these people, so an appointment should be easy to arrange. Professionals usually have discretionary income available to invest in outside projects, and if they're not interested, they may be able to recommend a colleague who is.
- *Business associates.* These are people you encounter during the normal course of your business day. Of course, you need to already be in business to use these possibilities. They can be divided into three subgroups:
    1. *Suppliers/vendors.* The owners of companies who supply your inventory and other needs have a vital interest in your company's success and make excellent angels. A supplier's investment may not come in the form of cash but in the form of better payment terms or cheaper prices. Suppliers might even use their credit to help you get a loan.
    2. *Customers.* These are especially good contacts if they use your product or service to make or sell their own goods. List all the customers with whom you have this sort of business relationship.
    3. *Employees.* There is no greater incentive to an employee than to share ownership in the company

for which they work. This can work very well if you open the opportunity for all employees to invest. If you only ask certain employees, you may create an awkward work environment with "vested" employees assuming they have additional privileges, which can wreck your work culture. Be careful.

- *Competitors.* These include owners of similar companies you don't directly compete with. If a competitor is doing business in another part of the country and does not infringe on your territory, they may be an empathetic investor and may share not only capital but information as well.

The nonaffiliated angels category includes:

1. *Professionals.* This group can include lawyers, accountants, consultants, and brokers whom you don't know personally or do business with.
2. *Middle managers.* Angels in middle management positions start investing in small businesses for three major reasons—either they're bored with their jobs and are looking for outside interests, they are nearing retirement, or they fear they are being phased out.
3. *Entrepreneurs.* These angels are (or have been) successful in their own businesses and like investing in other entrepreneurial ventures. Entrepreneurs who are familiar with your industry make excellent investors. This is often the most fertile group for finding angel investors.

How to Find Angel Investors

Because angels invest their own money, you might think they are the most discriminating, difficult-to-please investors. In fact, as a rule, they're much more willing to take a flier on a risky, unproven idea than are professional investors and lenders.

Give the People What They Want

Investors are looking for certain qualities in an entrepreneur. Among the most common are:

- Strong communication skills
- A comprehensive understanding of risk
- The willingness to take advice
- Market and operational adaptability
- Originality in the business idea
- A plan to execute your ideas

Angels often take a personal interest in a project and may simply believe strongly in the person behind it—that's you! They're usually swayed more by personal concerns than financial ones.

While angel investors used to be located primarily by word-of-mouth, they've become much easier to find in the electronic age. The Angel Capital Association (angelcapitalassociation.org) founded in 2004, is home to 14,000 angel investors. It's a great place to learn about angels and seek out an angel network—a local group of angel investors in your area.

Keep in mind that, above all else, angels are unconventional. Many have little training in evaluating business ideas. If 20 angels turn you down, it doesn't mean a thing. Keep on plugging away—meet more angels until you meet one who's intrigued by your business idea and impressed by your determination.

Unlike venture capitalists who are investing large sums of money and monitoring your every move, angel investors can be an excellent choice for launching a small business. Most angels tend to start small and see how you're doing before adding to the pot. One of the nicest things about the angel networks that have formed in recent years is that they can pool their resources, giving you a few angel investors in one place at one time. This also makes it easier when you're preparing to meet with angel investors. Rather than meeting one at a time, you can meet several in one angel network or even a couple who will spread the word around the network. This way, you can determine which investors are interested in your industry. You can also check out FundingPost (fundingpost.com) for angel events, or for a directory of angel groups, you can visit AngelList at (angel.co). Searching the web for new or smaller local groups is also advisable.

"Quality, quality, quality: Never waver from it, even when you don't see how you can afford to keep it up. When you compromise, you become a commodity and then you die."
        —Gary Hirshberg, founder of Stonyfield Farm Yogurt

If, however, you don't feel you are ready to seek out angel inves-tors or venture capitalists to fund your startup, other forms of funding are available. As mentioned earlier, you can also reach out to a SCORE mentor for valuable guidance with evaluating what forms of funding will be most appropriate for your new business venture.

TIP
Keep this in mind when crafting your pitch to angel investors: When angels reject a potential investment, it's typically because (1) they don't know the key people well enough, or (2) they don't believe the owner and management have the experience and talent to succeed. If you can prepare for such concerns before your pitch, your odds of getting an investment are better.

Getting the Money
Once you've found potential angels, how do you win them over? Angels look for many of the same things professional venture capitalists look for:

- *Strong management.* Does your management team have a track record of success and experience?
- *Proprietary strength.* Proprietary does not necessarily mean you must have patents, copyrights, or trademarks on all your products. It just means that your product or service should be unusual enough to grab consumers' attention.
- *Window of opportunity.* Investors look for a window of opportunity when your company can be the first in a market and grab the lion's share of business before others.
- *Market potential.* Investors prefer businesses with strong market potential. That means a restaurateur with plans to franchise stands a better chance than one who simply wants to open one local site.
- *Return on investment.* Most angels will expect a return of 20 to 25 percent over five years. However, they may accept a lower rate of return if your business has a lower risk.

If angels consider the same factors as venture capital companies, what is the difference between them? You have an edge with angels because many are not motivated solely by profit.

Particularly if your angel is a current or former entrepreneur, they may be motivated as much by the enjoyment of helping a young business succeed as by the money they stand to gain. Angels are more likely than venture capitalists to be persuaded by an entrepreneur's drive to succeed, persistence, and mental discipline. In other words, it's often more than just the numbers. This is why angels have invested in many Broadway shows; they love being part of the theatre community, knowing that only a few shows make big money.

AHA!

Angels invest in companies for reasons that often go beyond dollars and cents. As a result, your appeal must not only be financial, but also emotional. For example: "We need more than just dollars. We look at you as someone who can share a wealth of valuable experience as well." In the long run, that may be even more important than capital.

That is why it is important that your business plan convey a good sense of your background, experience, and drive. Your business plan should also address the concerns above and spell out the financing you expect to need from startup to maturity.

Be sure to spell out all the terms of the investment in a written agreement; get your lawyer's assistance here. How long will the investment last? How will return be calculated? How will the investment be cashed out? Detail the amount of involvement an angel will have in the business and how the investment will be legalized.

Examine the deal carefully for the possibility of the investor parlaying current equity or future loans to your business into controlling interest. Such a deal is not made in heaven and could indicate you are working with a devil in angel's garb.

CHAPTER 12

Looking for Loans

The Ins and Outs of Debt Financing

UNLIKE EQUITY FINANCING, where you sell part of your business to an investor, debt financing simply means receiving money in the form of a loan that you will have to repay. You can turn to many sources for debt financing, including banks, commercial lenders, credit unions, and even your personal credit cards.

Types of Loans

You don't need to pinpoint the exact type of loan you need before you approach a lender; they will help you decide what type of financing is best for your needs. However, you should have some general idea of the types of loans available so you will understand what your lender is offering.

A mind-boggling variety of loans are available, which is complicated by the fact that the same type of loan may have different terms at different banks. For instance, a commercial loan at one bank might be written with equal installments of principal and interest, while at another bank, the loan is written with monthly interest payments and a balloon payment of the principal.

Here is a look at how lenders generally structure loans, with common variations.

Line of Credit Loans

The most useful type of loan for small businesses is a line of credit. In fact, it's probably the one permanent loan arrangement all business owners should have with their bankers because it protects the business from emergencies and stalled cash flow. Line of credit loans are intended for inventory purchases and operating costs covering working capital and business cycle needs. They are not intended for equipment or real estate purchases.

A line of credit is a short-term loan that extends the cash available in your business's checking account to the upper limit of the loan contract. Every bank has its own method of funding, but essentially, an amount is transferred to the checking account of your business in order to cover checks. The business pays interest on the actual amount advanced, from the time it is advanced until it is paid back.

Line of credit loans usually carry the lowest interest rate a bank offers because they are seen as fairly low risk. Some banks even include a clause that gives them the right to cancel the loan if they think your business is in jeopardy. Interest payments are made monthly, and the principal is paid off at your convenience. It is wise to make payments on the principal often. Bankers may also call this a *revolving line of credit*, and they see it as an indication that your business is earning enough income.

Most line of credit loans are written for periods of one year and may be renewed almost automatically for an annual fee. Some banks require that your credit line be fully paid off for seven to 30 days each contract year. This period is probably the best time to negotiate.

Even if you don't need a line of credit loan now, talk to your banker about how to get one. To negotiate a credit line, your banker will want to see current financial statements, the latest tax returns, and a projected cash-flow statement.

Installment Loans

These loans are paid back with equal monthly payments covering both principal and interest. Installment loans may be written to meet all types of business needs. You receive the full amount when the contract is signed, and interest is calculated from that date to the final day of the loan. If you repay an installment loan before its final date, there will be no penalty and an appropriate interest adjustment.

Installment loan terms will always be correlated to their use. A business cycle loan may be written as a four-month installment loan from, say, September 1 until December 31 and would carry the low interest rate because the risk to the lender is under one year. Business cycle loans may be written from one to seven years, while real estate and renovation loans may be written for up to 21 years. An installment loan is occasionally written with quarterly, half-yearly, or annual payments when monthly payments are inappropriate.

FYI
Want to apply for a commercial real estate loan from the comfort of home? C-Loans.com analyzes your loan application against a database of 750 commercial mortgage lenders, then provides you with a list of 30 or so that are the best match. It's up to you to take it from there by calling the lenders or emailing your commercial loan request to them.

Balloon Loans
Though these loans are usually written under another name, you can identify them by the fact that the full amount is received when the contract is signed but only the interest is paid off during the life of the loan, with a "balloon" payment of the principal due on the final day.

Occasionally, a lender will offer a loan in which both interest and principal are paid with a single balloon payment. Balloon loans are usually reserved for situations when a business has to wait until a specific date before receiving payment from a client for its product or services. In all other ways, they are the same as installment loans.

Interim Loans

When considering interim loans, bankers are concerned with who will be paying off the loan and whether that commitment is reliable. Interim loans are used to make periodic payments to the contractors building new facilities when a mortgage on the building will be used to pay off the interim loan.

Secured and Unsecured Loans

Loans can come in one of two forms: secured or unsecured. When your lender knows you well and is convinced that your business is sound and the loan will be repaid on time, they may be willing to write an unsecured loan. Such a loan, in any of the aforementioned forms, has no collateral pledged as a secondary payment source should you default on the loan. The lender provides you with an unsecured loan because it considers you a low risk. As a new business, you are highly unlikely to qualify for an unsecured loan; it generally requires a track record of profitability and success.

A secured loan, on the other hand, requires collateral but generally has a lower interest rate than an unsecured loan. When a loan is written for more than 12 months, is used to purchase equipment, or does not seem risk-free, the lender will ask that the loan be secured by collateral. The collateral used, whether real estate or inventory, is expected to outlast the loan and is usually related to its purpose.

Because lenders expect to use the collateral to pay off the loan if the borrower defaults, they will value it appropriately. A $20,000 piece of new equipment will probably secure a loan of up to $15,000; receivables are valued for loans up to 75 percent of the amount due; and inventory is usually valued at up to 50 percent of its sale price.

TIP

Almost every loan has covenants. These are promises that borrowers make to lenders about their actions and responsibilities. A typical covenant specifies the amount of debt the borrower can take on in the future. If you want to see just how restrictive your loan will be, look at the covenants section of the loan agreement.

Letter of Credit

Typically used in international trade, this document allows entrepreneurs to guarantee payment to suppliers in other countries. The document substitutes the bank's credit for the entrepreneur's up to a set amount for a specified period.

Other Loans

Banks all over the country write loans, especially installment and balloon loans, under a myriad of names. They include:

- Term loans, both short- and long-term, according to the number of years they are written for
- Second mortgages where real estate is used to secure a loan; usually long-term, they're also known as equity loans
- Inventory loans and equipment loans for the purchase of, and secured by, either equipment or inventory
- Accounts receivable loans secured by your outstanding accounts
- Personal loans where your signature and personal collateral guarantee the loan, which you, in turn, lend to your business
- Guaranteed loans in which a third party—an investor, spouse, or the SBA—guarantees repayment
- Commercial loans in which the bank offers its standard loan for small businesses

Once you understand the different types of loans, you are better equipped for the next step: "selling" a lender on your business.

Sources of Financing

When seeking debt financing, where do you begin? Carefully choosing the lenders you target can increase your odds of success. Here is a look at various loan sources and what you should know about each.

Bank on It

Traditionally, the paperwork and processing costs involved in making and servicing loans have made the small loans most entrepreneurs seek too costly for big banks to administer. Put plainly, a loan under $25,000—the type many startups are looking for—may not be worth a big bank's time.

In recent years, however, the relationship between banks and small businesses has been improving as more and more banks realize the strength and importance of this growing market. With corporations and real estate developers no longer spurring so much of banks' business, lenders are looking to entrepreneurs to take up the slack.

Many major banks have added special services and programs for small businesses; others are streamlining their loan paperwork and approval process to get loans to entrepreneurs faster. On the plus side, banks are marketing to small businesses like never before. On the downside, the streamlining process often means that, more than ever, loan approval is based solely on numbers and scores on standardized rating systems rather than on an entrepreneur's character or drive.

AHA!
Federal, state, and local governments all offer their own financing programs designed especially for small business owners. These programs include low-interest loans, venture capital, and economic and scientific development grants. You can find reliable information on how and where to find these programs on the USA.gov website usa. gov/funding-options.

Second-String Funding Options

These three lesser-known funding options can provide incremental and critical startup capital:

1. **Equipment financing (aka asset-based or capital equipment loans).** With the equipment serving as baked-in collateral, equipment financing carries high approval rates for startups. One huge benefit: using the equipment to build equity while paying off the loan.

   How it works: Similar to a car loan, equipment typically provides 60 to 65 percent of its value as collateral. Interest rates are tied to your credit rating, and most borrowers aren't required to put up additional capital.

2. **Credit card cash advances.** Although interest rates can climb into the 20 percent territory, credit cards account for about seven percent of all startup capital. Those high interest rates make this a strategic option only for companies that can secure a lower-interest bank loan in the near term to pay them off.

   How it works: Say you have multiple credit cards with cash availability totaling $10,000 at 18 percent interest. You would take the maximum cash out and, after six months of credit-building, acquire a bank loan at 10 percent interest to pay them off.

3. **Merchant cash advance.** If you have a high volume of electronic transactions and need operating capital quickly, consider merchant cash advances. The capital comes at a steep price—as much as 50 percent interest—but it may be worth it if it keeps your doors open.

How it works: Specialized lenders provide cash in exchange for a percentage of all debit and credit card transactions over a defined period or until the loan is paid off. However, borrower beware: the merchant cash advance space is populated with sketchy lenders, making due diligence critical.

Given the challenges of working with a big bank, many entrepreneurs are taking a different tack. Instead of wooing the big commercial institutions, they are courting community banks where "relationship banking" is the rule, not the exception. It is easier to get a startup loan from community banks, according to Independent Community Bankers of America. They can be a little more flexible, don't have a bureaucracy to deal with, and are more apt to make character loans. Plus, they want to promote the local economy and show support for local businesses.

You'll still have to meet credit and collateral requirements just as you would at a larger institution. The difference: Smaller banks tend to give more weight to personal attributes. If the business is in town, the banker likely already knows the entrepreneur, and often the family has lived in the area for years. These things count more in a community bank.

Whether the bank you target is big or small, perhaps what matters most is developing relationships. If you have done your personal banking at the same place for 20 years and know the people with authority there, it makes sense to target that bank as a potential lender. If you do not have that kind of relationship at your bank, get to know bankers now. Visit chamber of commerce meetings, go to networking events, and take part in community functions that local bankers or other movers and shakers will attend.

Boost your chances of getting a loan by finding a lender whose experience matches your needs. Talk to friends, lawyers, or accountants, and other entrepreneurs in the same industry for leads on banks that have helped people in your business. Go online and research the local area banks. Check out local social media sites and introduce yourself as a new entrepreneur. This gives you an opportunity to meet neighbors whom you might not otherwise have had an opportunity to get to know. You can also make appointments with bank personnel, or even stop into a bank to talk about the type and size of loans they specialize in. Put in the work to find the right lender, and you'll find it is more likely to pay off.

Credit Card Financing Realities

"I've heard a lot of stories about startups that were floated on credit cards," says Paul Downs, author of *Boss Life: Surviving My Own Small Business* (Blue Rider Press, 2015). "But that's survivorship bias. No one pays any attention to the people who went down that road and didn't succeed. I'd imagine there are a lot more stories like that than the huge success stories."

The one benefit of using credit cards to finance a business is that it makes it easy to obtain financing. Why? Because credit card companies bank on you paying off credit card debt at high interest rates. Of course, this isn't a problem if you're able to pay off your balance in full every month. In fact, you get rewards from credit card use, and you can wait until the end of the month to pay for everything you've purchased to start the business. However, with the uncertainty and risk already involved in starting a business, you may want to ask yourself if this is something you want to take on. Should the business struggle, or even fail, you'll be stuck with debt for which you'll be personally responsible.

If you decide to get bank funding, being in credit card debt will hurt your chances. And if you are unable to pay off your credit cards in full each month, you can find yourself with cash-flow problems.

Moreover, according to www.creditcards.com, using credit cards for long-term expenses can be an expensive means of accessing cash: The average annual percentage rate on credit cards is 16.73 percent, which is roughly double what you'd pay for a loan backed by the SBA.

Mobile Banking

A vast number of individuals are using mobile banking. So are businesses, large and small.

The "J.D. Power 2019 U.S. Small Business Banking Satisfaction Study" found an 8 percent year-over-year increase in the percentage of small businesses that use their bank's mobile banking app. However, the "J.D. Power 2022 U.S. Small Business Banking Satisfaction Study" found that satisfaction declined among national bank mobile apps; credit card mobile apps; credit card websites; and regional bank mobile apps and websites.

Mobile banking saves time and money because you won't need to run to the bank all the time or spend money on mailing invoices or checks. It's much easier to conduct transactions electronically and check your account balances. Electronic banking also allows you to increase the rate of cash flowing through your company rather than waiting for transactions to be completed.

In many cases you can set up and customize your online banking experience. You can also do your banking at your own hours. This lets you pay bills electronically at your convenience, which will make life easier for you and those who handle your company's billing. As many people do with their home banking needs, you can also set up automated bill paying.

When considering a bank, you'll want to learn all about their mobile banking options and what features they offer. And as your company grows, you may need to assess the capabilities of your bank's online offerings. Many banks, including smaller ones, have a wealth of options. For any bank on your short list, make sure to also check reviews of the bank's mobile offerings on the internet.

And finally, there's security, which is so important today. The modern bank spends a great deal of time (and money) staying up-to-date on protecting the assets with which they are entrusted. Besides firewalls and encryption technology, banks are constantly updating antivirus and anti-malware detection software while staying on top of fraud, anomaly detection, potential identity theft, and password security.

Set up a meeting to discuss your needs and ask about security at your bank.

Commercial Finance Companies

Banks aren't your only option when seeking a loan. Nonbank commercial lenders, or commercial finance companies, have expanded their focus on small business in recent years as more and more small banks, which traditionally made loans to entrepreneurs, have been swallowed up in mergers. The advantage of approaching commercial finance companies is that, like community banks, they may be more willing to look beyond numbers and assets. Commercial finance companies give opportunities to startups and a lot of other businesses banks will not lend to. Here are two commercial finance companies to get you started:

1. Privately held *Commercial Finance Group* (cfgroup.net) specializes in providing finance solutions to small and midsize companies in a wide range of industries that are unable to qualify for bank financing.
2. At *Business Lenders* (businesslenders.com) loan evaluators look beyond traditional lending criteria to consider management ability and character. "Somebody who has bad credit could still be a good credit risk," says founder Penn Ritter. "It depends on why they had the credit problem."

Franchise Focus

Financing is any startup entrepreneur's biggest challenge—and it's no different for franchisees. The good news is franchisors may offer a little extra help in getting the capital you need.

Some franchisors offer direct financing to help franchisees with all or part of the costs of startup. This may take the form of equipment, real estate, or inventory financing. The goal is to free up money so franchisees have more working capital.

Many franchisors are not directly involved in lending but have established relationships with banks and commercial finance companies. Because these lenders have processed loans for other franchisees, they are more familiar with new franchisees' needs.

The franchisor you're interested in can tell you about any direct financing or preferred lender programs available. The Franchise Disclosure Document should also include this information.

If your franchisor doesn't have a preferred lender, you can often find financing by approaching banks that have made loans to other franchisees in the system. Talk to franchisees and see how they financed their businesses.

Once you've found a lender to target, you'll need to provide the same information and follow the same steps as you would with any type of business loan.

Commercial lenders require a business plan, personal financial statements, and cash-flow projections. They will usually expect you to come up with 20 to 25 percent of the needed capital yourself. For more information about commercial finance companies, visit Secured Finance Network at sfnet.com or call (212) 792-9390.

AHA!

Looking for financing? Consider an unexpected source—your vendors. Vendors may be willing to give you the capital you need, either through a delayed financing agreement or a leasing program. Vendors have a vested interest in your success and a belief in your stability, or they wouldn't be doing business with you. Before entering any agreement, however, compare long-term leasing costs with short-term loan costs; leasing is often more costly. Also consider your relationship with the vendor. If for some reason the products or services you are receiving from them fall short of their competitors, you may want to make a switch—but wait, you're in a different type of relationship now, which can make things tricky.

Give Yourself Credit

One potentially risky way to finance your business is to use your personal credit cards. The obvious drawback is the high interest rates; if you use the cards for cash advances rather than to buy equipment, the rates are even higher.

Some entrepreneurs take advantage of low-interest credit card offers they receive in the mail, transferring balances from one card to another as soon as interest rates rise (typically after six months). If you use this strategy, keep a close eye on when the rate will increase. Sometimes you can get the bank to extend the low introductory rate over the phone.

Experts advise using credit card financing as a last resort because interest rates are higher than any other type of financing. However, if you are good at juggling payments, your startup needs are low, and you are confident you'll be able to pay the money back fairly quickly, this could be the route to take. If you are skeptical about this approach, you should be. After all, as of 2020, an average household with a credit card carries $8,398 in credit card debt, and few of the folks in those households ever expected to go into debt—"it just happened." When you're financing a business, you can end up in this situation quickly. There is a reason why people separate their business and personal finances.

Applying for a Loan

The next step is applying for the loan. It's important to know what you'll need to provide and what lenders are looking for.

The Loan Application

Banks are in the money-lending business. To lend money, they need evidence of security and stability. It's that simple. How can you provide this evidence when your business hasn't even gotten off the ground? Begin by making sure your loan application is both realistic and optimistic. If you predict an increase in sales of between eight and 12 percent, explain how you can reach out to your market and generate enough sales to reach those numbers. Make sure you have all angles covered. Know your expenses, costs of doing business, your pricing, and how many products you expect to move or hours of service you can expect to do in a day, a week, a month, and a year. Be realistic and triple-check your math.

Also make sure your application is complete. When a piece of an application is missing, bankers instantly suspect that either something is being hidden or the applicant doesn't know their business well enough to pull the information together. Underwriting rules aren't as flexible as they used to be either.

There are 12 separate items that should be included in every loan application. The importance of each one varies with the size of your business, your industry, and the amount you are requesting.

1. Cover sheet
2. Cover letter
3. Table of contents
4. Amount and use of the loan
5. History and description of your business
6. Functions and background of your management team
7. Market information on your product or service
8. Financial history and current status
9. Financial projections to demonstrate that the loan will be repaid
10. A list of possible collateral
11. Personal financial statements
12. Additional documents to support the projections

"You fail if you don't try. If you try and you fail, yes, you'll have a few articles saying you've failed at something. But if you look at the history of American entrepreneurs, one thing I do know about them: an awful lot of them have tried and failed in the past and gone on to great things."
—Richard Branson, founder of the Virgin Group

Many of the items you'll be including in your loan application are part of your business plan; a few of them will have to be added. Here's a closer look at each section:

1. *Cover sheet.* This is the title page to your "book." All it needs to say is "Loan application submitted by John Smith, Sunday's Ice Cream Parlor, to Big Bucks Bank, Main Street, Anytown." It should also include the date and your business telephone number.

2. *Cover letter.* The cover letter is a personal business letter to your banker requesting consideration of your application for a line of credit or an installment loan. The second paragraph should describe your business: "Our company is a [sole proprietorship, partnership, or corporation] in manufacturing, distributing, and retailing X type of goods." The third paragraph is best kept to just one or two sentences that "sell" your application by indicating what your plans are for your business.

3. *Table of contents.* This page makes it easy for your banker to see that all the documents are included.

4. *Amount and use of the loan.* This page documents how much you want to borrow and how you will use the loan. If you are buying a new piece of equipment, for instance, it should show the contract price, add the cost of freight and installation, deduct the amount you will be contributing, and show the balance to be borrowed. Explain how and why this equipment is important for your business.

5. *History and description of your business.* This is often the most difficult to write. The key is to stay with the facts and assume the reader knows nothing about your business. Describe, more fully than in the cover letter, the legal form of your business and its location. Explain why you believe the business is going to succeed. Conclude with a paragraph on your future plans. If you have not yet started your business, which is probably the case with most people reading this book, it will be mostly about the latter . . . your future plans and predictions.

TIP

Loan officers at your bank may be a valuable resource in identifying state, local, and agency assistance. They may have gone through the steps with other new business owners in your area. Even if they don't offer you a loan, or a loan on terms you can accept, you should make time to chat and get their insights on other assistance.

6. *Management team.* Bankers know that people make things happen. Your management team might consist of every employee if they oversee an important part of your operation, or it might be just you and one key person. It also includes any outside consultants you plan to use regularly, such as your accountant or banker. In one or two pages, list each person's name and responsibilities. Where appropriate, describe the background that makes this person the right choice for that job. Also make sure that you have already included your own background, paying particular attention to anything that you have done that indicates that you are a good risk.

7. *Market information.* You should begin these pages with a complete description of your product line or service and

the market it is directed toward. Next, describe how you have targeted your market niche and how successful you have been. Finally, detail your future plans to add new products or services.

8. *Financial history.* Most bankers want to see balance sheets and income (profit and loss) statements. As a startup, you will need to use projections. Bankers will compare these to norms in your industry.

9. *Financial projections.* This set of three documents—a projected income statement, balance sheet, and cash-flow statement—should show how the business, with the use of the loan, will generate sufficient profits to pay off the loan. Your accountant can help you prepare these documents.

10. *Collateral.* Listing your available collateral—cash reserves, stocks and bonds, equipment, home equity, inventory, and receivables—demonstrates your understanding that your banker will normally look for a backup repayment source. Each piece of collateral listed should be described with its cost and current fair market value. You might need to provide documentation of value—so be prepared to get appraisals or get your paperwork in order.

AHA!
If you are a woman or a member of a minority group looking to purchase a franchise, you may be eligible for special financial incentives or assistance from the franchisor. Ask franchisors you are considering whether they have such programs and what the requirements are.

11. *Personal financial statements.* As a startup, you will need to add your personal guarantee to any loan the bank makes. The banker will want to see your tax returns for several years and balance sheets showing personal net worth.

Most banks have preprinted forms that make pulling these figures together relatively easy.

12. *Additional documents.* In this section, you can include whatever documents you feel will enhance your loan package. This might include a copy of the sales contract on a new piece of equipment, a lease and photograph of a new location, blueprints, or legal documents. If you are introducing a new product or service, include a product brochure and additional market research information.

This section can help a new business overcome the lack of a track record. While glowing letters won't make a banker overlook weak finances, an assurance from your largest customer that your services are valued can help your banker see your full potential.

As mentioned earlier, most of these sections come from your business plan.

WARNING

Be careful. A few years ago, *The Wall Street Journal* pointed out that some lenders, mostly those dealing with small-business loans, are combing through applicants' social media posts, tweets, and posted resumes. As social media continues to grow in popularity, more loan officers may check you out on social media platforms. So, it's a good idea to delete any posts, including photos, rants, off-color jokes, or inappropriate comments, that might be character-damaging. You'd be surprised by how your social media presence can be harmful in business, starting with business loans.

What Lenders Look For

Your application is complete, with every "i" dotted and every "t" crossed. But is it enough to get you the cold, hard cash? What are lenders really looking for when they pore over your application? Lenders typically base their decisions on four criteria, often called the "Four Cs of Credit":

1. *Credit.* The lender will examine your personal credit history to see how well you've managed your past obligations. If you have some black marks on your credit, the banker will want to hear the details and see proof that you repaid what you owed. A couple of late payments are not a big deal, but two or more consecutive missed payments are. Get a copy of your credit history before you turn in your application. This way, you can find out about any problems and explain them before your banker brings them up.

2. *Character.* Character is hard to measure, but lenders will use your credit history to assess this as well. They take lawsuits, bankruptcies, and tax liens particularly seriously in evaluating your character. They will also do a background check and evaluate your previous work experience. They might ask for personal references.

3. *Capacity.* What happens if your business slumps? Do you have the capacity to convert other assets to cash, either by selling or borrowing against them? Your secondary repayment sources may include real estate, stocks, and other savings. The lender will look at your business balance sheet and financial statement to determine your capacity.

4. *Collateral.* As a startup, you will most likely be seeking a secured loan. This means you must put up collateral— either personal assets, such as stocks or certificates of deposit, or business assets like inventory, equipment, or real estate.

Read the Fine Print

Hallelujah and yippee! You can almost hear the choirs of angels singing as your banker smiles and hands you the loan documents. You got the loan!

Not so fast. Before you sign that piece of paper, take a good look at what you're getting into. Many entrepreneurs are so excited about having their loans approved, they fail to read the fine print on their loan agreements. That can lead to trouble later on.

It's a good idea to get the loan documents ahead of time so you have a chance to review them for a couple of days before you sign, according to the American Bankers Association. Bankers won't have a problem sending advance copies of the documents but will generally do so only if they're specifically asked.

Most bankers will be happy to help you understand the fine print, but it's also a good idea to have your accountant and lawyer review the documents too. Let us repeat: *read* every word. And for any passages or terms you don't completely understand, get clarification from an accountant, lawyer, or trusted mentor who has experience understanding loan terms.

Although it varies slightly from bank to bank, a small business loan package usually consists of several documents, typically including a loan agreement, a promissory note, and some form of guarantee and surety agreement.

- **Loan agreement.** This specifies, in essence, the promises you are making to the bank and asks you to affirm that you are authorized to bind your business to the terms of the loan. Most banks require you to verify that all the information on your loan application is still true before they disburse the loan.

- **Promissory note.** This details the principal and interest owed and when payments are due. It outlines the events that would allow the bank to declare your loan in default. Knowing these events ahead of time can help you protect your credit record. Look for "cure" language in the default section. A cure provision allows you a certain amount of time (usually 10 days) to remedy the default after you've been notified by the bank. If such a provision isn't included, ask if it can be added to prevent you from defaulting accidentally (in case a payment is lost in the mail, or for some reason the electronic transfer did not go through). Also make sure you understand what the bank can and can't do after declaring default.

- **Guarantee and surety agreement.** Because startups generally have insufficient operating history or assets on which to base a loan, banks usually require the loan to be guaranteed with your personal assets. The bank may ask you to secure the loan with the equity in your home, for example.

A Loan at Last

A good relationship with your banker is just as important after you get that loan as it is in getting one in the first place. The keyword is "communication." The bank wants to be told all the good—and bad—news about your business as soon as it occurs. Most business owners fear telling bankers bad news, but keeping problems hidden is a mistake. Like any relationship, the one with your banker is built on trust. Keep them apprised of the progress of your business. Invite your banker to visit your business and see how the proceeds of the loan are being put to good use.

Once you've established a relationship with a banker, it is simple to expand your circle of friends at the bank. Every time you visit, spend some time meeting and talking to people, especially those further up the ladder. Often, the bankers will be the ones to initiate contact. Take advantage of this opportunity. The more people you know at the bank, the easier it will be to get the next round of financing.

PART 4
Bonus Section: Launching

CHAPTER 13

Looking Good

Creating a Professional Image

THESE DAYS, IT IS JUST NOT ENOUGH to sell terrific products, offer super service, and have a solid business plan to back you up. Your company image is equally important to the overall success of your business.

Every time you send your business card or an email, write a press release, or welcome a client into your office or store, or greet them on Zoom, you are selling someone on your company. Even the look of your office helps "sell" your business by conveying an image, whether it is that of a funky, creative ad agency or a staid, respectable accounting firm.

Your logo, website, business card, signage, landing pages, and style are all part of a cohesive image program known as *corporate identity*. And with the right corporate identity, your company can appear highly professional and give the impression of having been in business for years, even if you are brand-new.

In this chapter, we will discuss how to create a corporate image that works.

Office Space

How you set up your office depends on what you are using it for and who's going to see it. If you're working from home, perhaps running an online business, your customers won't see your office, so your goal should simply be to make it as functional as possible for your needs. Perhaps you'll just need a well-chosen backdrop for video calls, conferencing, and Zoom meetings (Zoom even lets you choose backdrops). As for furnishings, you can do it on the cheap with whatever you find that's useful.

If, however, your business will require an office in which you will meet clients and vendors, and have employees, you need something more professional and practical. Your design should reflect who you are and what you do. If you're meeting clients to whom you are going to be giving golf lessons, your office won't be formal but may instead have casual furnishings and be decorated with golfing photos and even trophies that you've won. If your office is in your high-end luxury furniture store, it should be outfitted with the furnishings you sell. Office space says a lot about the business you're in, so make it a representation of your business.

It's also important that you factor in office space for employees. In the virtual world, they have the luxury of decorating their own home offices, but if your business is in an office building or even in the back office of a retail store, you will need to provide basic amenities for your employees. You don't need to spend a ton of money, but you will want to make the office aesthetically pleasing as well as comfortable and functional for the people who will be working there.

What's in Store?

Got a retail location? Ask yourself these questions to make sure your store has the "eye appeal" it needs to keep customers coming back:

- Are your shelves clean and neat? Is merchandise displayed so people can see it easily?
- Is the area around your cash registers or terminals clean and orderly?
- Can you find forms, packaging, and related materials quickly and easily?
- Are light fixtures clean, bright, and working properly?

- Is there plenty of room between counters and shelves so that aisles are wide and free of barriers?
- Are glass surfaces clean and floors vacuumed or swept and scrubbed regularly?

Everything in Its Place

Improving your own and your employees' performance involves a lot more than finding comfortable chairs. It involves the placement of offices or cubicles within the building, proximity to equipment, and lighting, desk space, meeting areas, privacy, and more. If people are going to be spending most of their waking hours at your company's office, it should be designed in a manner that helps maximize production while also promoting teamwork. The right design can have a tremendous effect on morale.

"When I see a barrier, I cry and I curse, and then I get a ladder and climb over it."

—John Johnson, founder of Johnson Publishing Co.

How can you create a high-performance office? The first step is addressing organizational issues of who sits where. The days of big "power desks" and hierarchical corner offices are over. More businesses are turning to flexible environments ideal for small companies where the business owner probably doubles as salesperson. Indeed, many large companies have even done away with offices for executives, instead giving them the window seat on a long row of desks at which everyone who works for the company busily works away.

Regardless, with today's emphasis on team-building, office design is moving away from compartmentalized offices and moving toward spaces where employees can work. When setting up your space, think about who needs to work with whom and which employees share what resources. If you group those people together, you enhance their productivity. And if you're more visible and accessible, you'll be more plugged into any daily concerns or challenges that you can tackle before they become real problems.

In addition to maximizing your own and your employees' productivity, your office may also function as a marketing tool if clients or customers visit. Think about what visitors will see when they come by. Will they be bombarded with noise from one department near the entrance? Or will they see a series of closed doors with seemingly no activity taking place? Visitors should not be overwhelmed by chaos as they walk through your building, but they should see signs of life and get glimpses of the daily activities going on at your company.

Your customers should get a vibe that tells them this is where they want to be, where they want to do business. How you convey that depends on your business type and the expectations your customers have walking in the door. A quiet coffee shop might be best with soft couches and light music playing at the entrance, while a cutting-edge marketing and advertising company catering to startups might need a more visual wow factor and some hustle and bustle upon entrance.

On the Outside

If you will be entertaining clients and others in your office, you'll also want to concern yourself with outside appearance. If the first impression a potential customer has of your business is a shabby door or an unkempt parking lot, you're not sending the right message . . . and all your hard work in designing an attractive, efficient office could be going to waste.

Step outside your place of business and take a long, hard look at the parking lot, sidewalks, windows, exterior lighting, landscaping, and the exterior of the building. A well-maintained building projects an industrious, professional image. Weeds, trash, broken sidewalks, tattered awnings, dirty windows, dead plants, and overflowing trash containers send the message "We don't care." It might also turn off customers or clients who are wary of entering a location that seems unsafe, desolate, or just unkempt.

Whether you're in a retail location or an office building, take the time to check the property from the outside. If you own the property, take it upon yourself to make some changes. If you are renting or leasing, you can contact your landlord and ask for some changes. You want to make sure people are comfortable visiting your office.

TIP

Evaluate business card designs with these criteria in mind:
- Is the card easy to read?
- Does the design catch your eye? (A good designer can make even an all-type card appealing.)
- Is your name and the name of your business immediately identifiable?
- Is all your contact information easy to see, including your website, email address, phone number, and address if people will be coming to your business in person?

Designing a Logo

Before you start designing a business card or picking colors for your letterhead, you need a logo. Featuring your company name, embellished with a little color and perhaps a few graphic touches here and there, your logo is the most important design element because it is a visual representation of your business. It is a focal point that appears on packaging, signage, promotional materials, emails, stationery, and your business cards.

Through the use of color and graphics, your logo should reflect the overall image you want your company to convey. It should give people a feel for what your company is all about—and give them a sense of what they can expect from you.

For example, say your product is an organic face cream you will be marketing to health-conscious consumers. Your logo should represent your product's best benefits—being all-natural and environmentally sound. Creating a simple, no-nonsense logo using earth tones and a plain typeface will give the impression of a product that is "back to basics," which is exactly what you want to achieve. Take that same product and give it a slick, high-tech look with neon colors, however, and people won't associate your logo with the down-to-earth product you're selling.

Secrets to Making Your Logo Stand Out

If asked, most of us could name at least a few iconic logos, whether it is Coca-Cola's cursive script, the charging bull of Merrill Lynch, or Nike's Swoosh. That's the point—having a logo that stays in the minds of those who see it. "Other people have to be able to speak for your brand," says Jonah Berger, author of *Contagious: Why Things Catch On* (Simon & Schuster, 2013) and a marketing professor at the Wharton School of the University of Pennsylvania. "You love your company, you think your company is great, but if you're not around, what are people going to remember? And what are they going to tell others?"

The best logos have several things in common. Here are Berger's five keys to a successful logo:

1. **Simplicity.** "A good way to think about simplicity is how many moving pieces are in the logo," Berger says. For instance, the old Apple logo was rainbow-colored, while the current one is rendered in solid black or simple grayscale. That newfound simplicity makes the logo easy to look at, which customers appreciate. "The easier it is to process things, the more we like those things." For that reason, most brands want to present a simple aesthetic that is easy for consumers to digest.

2. **Brand consistency.** Your logo will communicate things to consumers about your brand, so you need to ensure that its design fits your company's overall message. Consider the Apple logo again. A few decades ago, Berger says, "rainbow colors had a certain association [with] being free and easygoing," but not anymore. While Apple's old logo connoted the free spirit of an upstart that was taking on staid tech giants, its current position as one of the most valuable corporations in the world calls for the sleek, futuristic logo it has now. "That's consistent with the message that Apple wants to suggest: we are technology, but we're friendly technology; we're easy-to-use technology." If you're starting a new company, Berger says, you should put some serious thought into your brand's key characteristics and how you want to convey them in your logo.

3. **Memorability.** Memorability is the quality that makes your logo easy for customers to recall, which leads to repeat customers and word-of-mouth, says Berger. Your logo should "help them remember that you exist and what you stand for," he says.

4. **Remarkability.** The remarkability of a logo is what makes it "worthy of remark," cutting through the clutter of your industry to reach customers, Berger says. "If you're an established brand, you may not want a remarkable logo. But if you're a startup, you need to take a little more risk."

5. **Market testing.** Don't just trust your gut when designing a logo, Berger says. Do market research. One way to test various logo designs is to put out a survey on a service such as Amazon's Mechanical Turk. "We could throw up a quick study for an entre-preneur for $10, and within a day get a lot of feedback from different people about how heavy or light, fast or slow, a logo would be," Berger says. The point is not to assume that a given logo is great. Get some independent feedback about whether your logo is saying everything you want it to say.

Logos come in two basic forms: abstract symbols (like the apple in Apple Inc.) or logotypes, a stylized rendition of your company's name. Consider Allstate's "good hands" logo. It immediately generates a warm feeling for the company, symbolizing care and trust. It's a good use of an abstract symbol matched with the brand. In the case of McDonald's golden arches, they serve not only as a symbol, but the yellow arches are literally what you will see from the highway to indicate a McDonald's is nearby. The logo serves as a point of reference.

But beware of going too abstract: "Such a symbol is meaningless until your company can communicate to consumers what its underlying associations are," says Americus Reed II, a marketing professor at the University of Pennsylvania's Wharton School, who's conducted research on the triggers that lead consumers to identify with and become loyal to a brand.

The logos of IBM, Microsoft, and Sony, on the other hand, use type treatments with a twist that makes them distinctive. You can also use a combination of both. Alan Siegel, former chairman of Siegel+Gale, a design firm specializing in corporate identity, warns that promoting an abstract symbol can prove costly for a small business on a budget. In addition, he says, such logos are harder to remember. "A logotype or word mark is much easier to recall," says Siegel. "If you use an abstract symbol, always use it in connection with your business name."

You may also want to consider creating several sample logos with artificial intelligence (AI) apps to see what would suit you. These include Dall-E-2, Midjourney, and DreamStudio (Stable Diffusion). But, even if you have a good eye for color and a sense of what you want your logo to look like, you may still want to consult a professional designer. Why? They will typically know whether a logo design will transfer easily onto mobile devices, into print, or onto a sign. Your logo is the foundation for all your promotional materials, so this is one area where spending a little time and money now pays off later.

Business Cards

Once you have your logo, it's time to apply it to the marketing items you will use most, such as business cards. A good business card should convey the overall image of your business—not easy, considering the card measures only two inches by three inches. How can you possibly get a message across in such a small amount of space?

You can't expect your business card to tell the whole story of your company. What you should expect it to do is present a professional image people will remember. "A business card can make or break a client's first impression of your company," says Evenson.

The color, wording, and texture of your business card have a lot to do with its appeal and its ability to convey your company image. Use common sense when you are designing your business card. If your business markets children's toys and games, you might try using bright and primary colors. You could put the written words in a child's script, but of course, it's the grown-ups who have to read it—so don't overdo it. On the other hand, if you run a financial consulting service, then you want your business card to convey professionalism and reliability, so stick to traditional looks, such as black printing on a gray, beige, or white background.

AHA!

Ask owners of noncompeting but related businesses if you can display some of your business cards on their counters. A pet sitter, for example, could leave their business cards on the counter at a pet store. Offer to do the same for them.

Multiple inexpensive printing services, such as Vistaprint (vistaprint.com), Moo (moo.com), and Zazzle (zazzle.com) offer ideas and basic design templates. Their online tools can be just the ticket for creating a card when you have an idea in mind and a logo in hand. The best course of action: look at all the business cards you receive and emulate the cards you like. You have more leeway if you are in a creative business, such as party planning or retailing, but in general, keep the following tips in mind:

- Keep it simple. Do not cram too much information on the card.
- Do include the essentials—your name, title, company name, address, phone and fax numbers, and email and website addresses.
- Make the typeface easy to read.
- Stick to one or two colors.
- Include your logo if you have one.

Once you've got business cards, make the most of them:

- Always give people more than one card (so they can give it to others).
- Include your card in all mailings.
- Carry cards with you at all times in a card case so they're clean and neat.

In the Cards

Business cards don't have to be boring. If your industry allows for a little creative flair, here are some ideas to try.

- Perhaps you'll want to include a photo of you if you're a service provider, or a product if you sell products, or perhaps a beautiful skyline as a backdrop if you help people with their travel plans to major cities. Choose the photo to suit your needs.
- Although they are more expensive than standard business cards, cards in nontraditional shapes get attention. Try a teddy bear shape for a day-care service, for example, or a birthday cake for a party planner.

Just make sure it still fits in the standard wallet—if people can't get your card into their wallet, they will toss it.

- Textured paper can add to a card's interest (make sure it does not detract from readability, though) as can colored paper. In general, stay with lighter shades that enhance readability.
- Thermography, a process that creates raised, shiny print, adds interest to a card. Embossing and foil stamping are two other printing processes that can give your card visual appeal.

Designing Your Sign

Retailers and restaurateurs alike realize the power of a good sign. Some companies rely on drive-by or walk-by traffic for customers, and if that's the case with your company, your sign may be the most important element of your entire corporate identity.

A good sign must do more than just attract attention; it also has to be readable from a distance. That's why your logo is so important—one that looks great on a tiny business card may not transfer well to a huge sign above your store. Clearly, going to a professional in the first stages of developing your image is essential. If you find out your great logo can't be reproduced on a sign, you'll have to go back to square one and rethink it, which will end up costing you more in the long run.

In recent years, a whole host of new signage materials has emerged to provide more variety and individuality. This also means it's harder to choose among all the possibilities, which include neon, plastic, metal, wood, and more. Do some investigating before making your final decision; there is a wide range of prices for various materials. Depending on your location, sign placement can make a big difference, too. Options include a freestanding sign, a wall sign, a projecting sign, or a roof sign.

Before you head to a sign manufacturer with your design specifications, check your local zoning laws. You may find that the design you've come up with for your fried chicken restaurant—a

30-foot neon number in the shape of a chicken—isn't allowed in your area. If you are moving into a shopping center, the developer may have additional regulations governing signage that can be used in the facility.

Most entrepreneurs typically know little about creating signs. For example, you probably will not know how big the letters should be to be visible from down the block, and you may not know which materials fare best in inclement weather. For this reason, you should visit a professional—either a designer or a sign fabricator. A good designer knows when fabricators are cutting corners and not using the material requested or doing a shoddy job. A designer will also be present at the time of installation to make sure the sign is properly installed.

The cost of a sign varies greatly depending on the materials, type of sign, and whether it's lighted. Buying directly from a fabricator can cost as little as $500, but you run the risk of not meeting zoning requirements. If you hire a designer, you'll pay a design fee in addition to fabrication costs, but you have a better guarantee that the finished product will work for you. Oh, and always proofread your sign before it's fabricated. A typo isn't just embarrassing—remaking a sign will cost you.

CHAPTER 14

Staffing Smarts

Hiring Employees

TO HIRE OR NOT TO HIRE? THAT IS THE QUESTION in the mind of the new entrepreneur. You see, hiring even one employee changes everything. Suddenly, you need payroll procedures, rules regarding hours, and a policy for vacation pay. You're hit with a multitude of legal requirements and management duties you'd never have to deal with if you worked solo.

To decide whether you need employees, take a closer look at your ultimate goals. Do you want to create the next Starbucks, or do you simply want to work on your own terms? If your goals are modest, then adding a staff may not be the best solution for you.

If you do need employees, there are plenty of ways to meet your staffing needs—without driving yourself nuts. From temporaries and independent contractors to employee leasing, this chapter takes a closer look at the dos and don'ts of staffing your business.

How to Hire

The employees you hire can make or break your business. While you may be tempted to hire the first person who walks in the door "just to get it over with," doing so can be a fatal error. A small company cannot afford to carry deadwood on staff, so start smart by taking time to figure out your staffing needs before you even begin looking for job candidates.

The first thing to ask yourself is why you are hiring people. You don't hire simply to have people around to talk to; you hire because you have business needs. For example, you can bring in employees to take over some of your responsibilities so you can free up more of your own time to grow the business. In other instances, you may have various needs from day one that you cannot handle by yourself, such as waiting on customers, creating products, or making sales. Covering some of the tasks you cannot do yourself and freeing yourself up to grow the business are two important reasons for hiring. You may also need employees to handle jobs that are out of your area of expertise. It's important to know what you do not excel at and find someone (or several people) to handle those jobs. As they say, "Know what you don't know."

Start by making a list of those responsibilities for which you need to hire people. For example, if you're opening a restaurant and you're not a chef, you'll need to hire one, along with servers, kitchen help, and a host or hostess. In office settings you may need administrative assistants, a bookkeeper, and so forth.

List the responsibilities of each task and think about where it can be performed. If space is tight, hiring remote workers is an option. In recent years, more and more jobs are being performed remotely. However, you need to hire remote workers you can trust to get the work done without supervision.

FYI

Use the internet to help you find employees:

- **CareerBuilder** (careerbuilder.com) offers advice, webinars, leadership development, and hiring solutions to employers and job recruiters.
- **Monster** (monster.com) helps you screen resumes so you can find the right candidate quickly.
- **Indeed** (www.indeed.com) and ZipRecruiter (www.ziprecruiter. com) give you more exposure to job seekers as the former is

the top jobs site by traffic and the latter will target candidates in its resume bank that fit your job description.
- **LinkedIn** (linkedin.com) is also a place where employers go to search for and recruit professional employees.

Job Analysis

Begin by understanding the requirements of each job being filled. What kind of skills, abilities, personality, experience, and education are needed? To determine these attributes, sit down and do a job analysis covering the following areas:

- The physical/mental tasks involved (ranging from judging, planning, and managing to cleaning, lifting, and welding)
- How the job will be done (the methods and equipment used)
- The reason the job exists (including an explanation of how the job affects other positions in the company)
- The qualifications needed (training, knowledge, skills, and personality traits)

If you are having trouble, one good way to get information for a job analysis is to talk to employees and supervisors at other companies that have similar positions.

The job description is basically an outline of how the job fits into the company. It should point out in broad terms the responsibilities and duties. First, write down the job title and to whom that person will report. Next, develop a job statement or summary describing what the individual will need to do and how their activities relate to other positions in the company. Determine to whom each person will report, and who will report directly to you. Hint: When you're starting out, your first employees, if possible, should report to you until you see which ones have the aptitude to manage others.

For a one-person business hiring its first employee, these

steps may seem unnecessary, but remember, you are laying the foundation for your personnel policy, which will be essential as your company grows. Keeping detailed records from the time you hire your first employee will make things a lot easier when you hire your 50th.

TIP

It's easy to hire employees who are just like you, but it's often a mistake. Especially with your first employee, try to find someone who complements your strengths and weaknesses. While personal compatibility is important, hiring a carbon copy of yourself could leave your business ill-prepared for challenges. Look for people who are attentive, listen to you, and can work independently. In the beginning, employees will have a lot of questions until they get the lay of the land, but you want people who you do not have to micromanage. Remember, the whole idea of having employees is so they can do the things you do not have the time, skills, or experience to handle. Hopefully, you will find people who bring in some fresh ideas that will enhance what you and your company want to accomplish.

Job Specification

The job specification describes the personal requirements you expect from the employee. Like the job description, it includes the job title, to whom the person reports, and a summary of the position. However, it also lists any educational requirements, desired experience, and specialized skills or knowledge required. Include salary range and benefits. Finish by listing any physical or other special requirements associated with the job as well as any occupational hazards.

Writing the job description and job specification will also help you determine whether you need a part- or full-time employee, whether the person should be permanent or temporary, and whether you could use an independent contractor to fill the position (more on all these options later).

AHA!

For higher level positions, you can also sign up with a headhunter. Typically, headhunters are reserved for higher paying positions, and they make their money by taking a percentage of the first year's salary that you offer the client.

Writing Job Ads

There are numerous websites on which you can post jobs, as well as classified sections of online and print publications. But before you place an ad anywhere, research what other ads on the website or in the newspaper look like. Notice how they are positioned, presented, and the amount of space you are afforded, which will vary from one place to another. In most cases, you will have a form in which to include much of the job information. Use the job specification and description to fill out the form or write an ad that will attract candidates to your company. The best way to avoid wasting time on interviews with people who do not meet your needs is to write an ad that will lure qualified candidates and discourage others. Consider this example:

> Interior designer seeks inside/outside salesperson. Flooring, drapes (extensive measuring), furniture, etc. In-home consultations. Competitive salary plus commission. Minimum two years' experience. San Francisco Bay Area. Email resume to (put company or your own email address) or mail to (use company address).

This job description is designed to attract a flexible salesperson while making it clear that commission is part of the payment process. Anyone who is not confident working on commission should not apply. The advertiser asks for expertise in "extensive measuring," which is an important/specific skill necessary for the position. The job location should be included. If the job can be performed remotely, you should include that if it is a possibility.

If you use an online job portal, you need to understand how they operate and what you will have to pay. "Free postings" doesn't mean you won't have to pay a fee. Sites like Indeed, for example, charge by how many people click on your ad. If someone clicks on your ad, you may pay between $.25 and $1.50, or more. This is why you want your ad to be as specific as possible so you don't incur extra costs when tons of people click on the ad, who either don't have the credentials for the position or who want a higher pay rate than you wish to pay. Other sites may charge you by how many candidates you interview. The point is that places like Monster, Indeed, Naukri, and others make money from employer listings. These are among the major players in job hunting, and you should allot a portion of your budget to staffing if you plan to use them.

Here are a few online listings to give you an idea of how they look:

Salary
$25–$30 an hour

Full Job Description
The Food Bank of Central & Eastern (state) is an exciting, challenging, and rewarding place to work. Our vision: No one goes hungry. Mission: Nourish people. Build solutions. Empower communities. We are an equal opportunity employer and are known for our core values of Respect, Integrity, Compassion, Dedication, Teamwork, and Fun!

Real Estate Sales: Connecticut

Full Job Description
We're looking for an experienced real estate inside sales agent
to play a key role on our team. The ideal applicant has a knack
for identifying sales opportunities, generating qualified leads,
and funneling them to our buyers and listing agents.

If you're driven to achieve success, love developing relationships with clients over the phone, have a strong work ethic, and
have a desire to control your income, then please apply!

Compensation:
Starting at $50,000
Responsibilities:
- Qualify the incoming leads you generate for appointments with
  realtors and field agents to provide quick response times and
  meet their needs.
- Produce sales reports on a monthly and quarterly basis to make
  sure all sales goals are met.
- Contact prospects after the initial meeting via phone calls, email,
  and other forms of communication to add them to the sales pipe-
  line and cultivate real estate qualified leads.
- Develop new business opportunities within specific geographies
  to expand clientele.
- Put up-to-date information on clients into the database system
  so agents have the most accurate and current data.
Qualifications:
- Over one year of experience generating real estate leads
- High school diploma, bachelor's degree desired
- Superb interpersonal and communication skills
- Valid U.S. driver's license with the ability to travel by car
- Valid real estate license
- Familiarity with (*list neighborhoods*)

You might also include some background on your business and a date by which candidates must apply.

To write a similarly targeted ad for your business, look at your job specifications and pull out the top four or five skills that are most essential to the job. Don't, however, list requirements other than educational or experience-related ones in the ad. Nor should you request specific personality traits (such as outgoing, detail-oriented) because people are likely to come in and imitate those characteristics when they don't really possess them. Instead, you should focus on telling the applicants about the excitement and challenge of the job, the salary, and what is expected of them. Finally, specify how applicants should contact you.

You might also consider including a few sentences about what makes your company's culture stand out. In this day and age, many applicants look for a strong cultural fit alongside job fit, opportunity for advancement, and compensation.

Recruiting Employees

The obvious first choice for recruiting employees is the internet; it's where people go to find a multitude of things, even jobs. As mentioned earlier, the leading job websites are Indeed, Monster, ZipRecruiter, FlexJobs, CareerBuilder, and other portals, along with the social media site LinkedIn. Many portals offer support and resources, such as articles, links to books, or resume-building tools, to help you facilitate your needs.

Meet the Expert: Caroline Stokes, CEO of FORWARD, Executive Coach, and Author

Caroline Stokes is CEO of FORWARD, an executive headhunter, Marshall Goldsmith Thinkers50 Award Winning Executive Coach, and author of *Elephants Before Unicorns: Emotionally Intelligent HR Strategies to Save Your Company* (Entrepreneur Press, 2019).

What are the first steps a business owner should take when hiring a new employee?

You've evaluated how you need to grow your product and your company. You know what culture you want to grow into. How exciting! Next, review your pain points and growth plans. Evaluate your culture so you can be transparent with the people you interview to see if they want to be a part of your organization's mission and culture development. They need to be on board with that so they can integrally support the big vision. If you hide behind cultural expectations, you will be virtue signaling and you'll never understand why you couldn't get your ideal hire.

If you haven't hired for this position before, simply get inspired by Googling other job descriptions in the market. Review the job description's language. Have other people review it too so they can see the connective tissue between your website presence, how your product serves and will evolve, and how your people are integral to that mission.

Then A/B test the job ad, or you are going to headhunt people with your job description via LinkedIn. I'm a headhunter and I can tell you that you can hire your most important people yourself if you spend a day strategically evaluating people via LinkedIn before sending people your job description.

Next, get feedback from the prospective candidates. The feedback will hurt. They will perhaps want higher compensation and bigger benefits, or they won't leave their secure job because they have a spouse and children to support. This is where your mission must so intoxicatingly resonate with the people you want to join you in your rocket ship that those barriers aren't even an issue anymore.

What is the most important factor to consider when hiring?

The most important factor in the person you're hiring will be the compatibility to deliver on the requirements of the role, emotional intelligence, and their ability to adapt in a new environment. Just because a person has emotional intelligence doesn't mean they are competent at what they do. A person who is competent at what they do but alienates, harasses, or lacks care in the way they communicate, connect, and influence will fail.

As the person hiring the right people on your rocket ship, you've got a lot of heavy lifting to do to evaluate the right person for the job, and how in tune they are with your company's preferred behavioral operating system.

How important is finding a "cultural fit" for your team?

We all want our new, hopeful hires to synchronize well with the team. When it doesn't work out, we're often confused, and that can impact future decision-making confidence.

If you have several or many employees, have them talk through a workplace diagnostic; you're going to understand very quickly whether you create a safe place, or if everyone is just plain happy with the status quo. Take the data and adapt quickly. If you're in a competitive environment, you need to build on every aspect of your employee experience.

When interviewing talent, you'll have those frank conversations too. It's like dating: If you aren't up-front about who you are and what respectful behavior looks like, you'll probably end up with a messy divorce.

In the pre-internet days, the classified ad section of the local newspaper was the number one place for job hunters, and many still offer listings in their printed and online versions. Place your ad in the Sunday or weekend edition of the largest-circulation local papers. It's still a good resource, particularly for lower-level and entry-level positions.

"My philosophy is, 'When you snooze, you lose.' If you have a great idea, at least take the chance and put your best foot forward."
—Ron Popeil, founder of Ronco Inventions LLC

Job hunting requires a multifaceted approach, which means as an employer you should also avoid putting all your eggs in one basket. You can use plenty of other methods besides the internet and newspapers to recruit good employees. Here are some ideas:

- *Contact school placement offices.* List your openings with trade and vocational schools, colleges, universities, and perhaps graduate schools. Check with your local school board to see if high schools in your area have job training and placement programs.
- *Post notices at senior citizen centers.* Retirees who need extra income or a productive way to fill their time can make excellent employees.
- *Use an employment agency.* Private and government-sponsored agencies can help with locating and screening applicants. Often, their fees are more than justified by the amount of time and money you save.
- *List your opening with an appropriate job bank.* Many professional associations have job banks for their members. Contact groups related to your industry, even if they are outside your local area, and ask them to alert their members to your staffing needs.
- *Use industry publications.* Trade association newsletters and industry publications often have classified ad sections where members can advertise job openings. This is an effective way to attract skilled people in your industry.
- *Word-of-mouth.* Mention that you are looking for someone at your next chamber of commerce meeting, at your weekly poker game, or while watching your kid's next soccer game. Talk about your job needs on local social media sites or in online groups, if allowed by the (often overly strict) group administrators. The point is to spread the word. And when you have employees, provide a cash incentive if they find you a candidate you end up hiring. It's all about networking, which saves you time and money, and often produces the best candidates. Just make sure you provide accurate information and the best way to

contact you. But a word of warning: don't hire anyone as a favor unless you know they are a good fit for the position.

TIP

If relevant, ask employees to send samples of their work with their resumes or to bring them to the interview. Another technique: Ask them to complete a project similar to the actual work they'd be doing (and pay them for it). This gives you a strong indication of how they would perform on the job . . . and them a clear picture of what you expect.

Prescreening Candidates

Three important tools in prescreening job candidates are the resume, the employment application, and the social media profile(s). If you ask applicants to send in a resume, that will be the first tool you use to screen them. You will then have qualified candidates fill out an application when they come in for an interview. And you can then get more information about them from their LinkedIn profile.

In any case, it is important to have an application form ready before you begin the interview process. You can buy generic application forms at most office supply stores or online, or you can develop your own to meet your specific needs. Make sure any application form you use conforms to Equal Employment Opportunity Commission (EEOC) guidelines regarding questions you can and cannot ask.

Your application should ask for specific information, such as name, address, and phone number; educational background; work experience, including salary levels; awards or honors; whether the applicant can work full or part time, as well as available hours; and any skills relevant to the job (foreign languages, familiarity with software programs, and so on.). If your job is located in the United States, you will also want to know if the applicant is an American citizen or has the appropriate paperwork to work in this country.

Be sure to ask for names and phone numbers of former supervisors to check as references; if the candidate is currently employed, ask if it is OK to contact their current place of employment. You may also want to ask for personal references. Because many employers these days hesitate to give out information about an employee, you may want to have the applicant sign a waiver that states the employee authorizes former and/or current employers to disclose information about them. Even when you have that waiver, some employers have policies that only allow them to confirm employment dates—and some have even stricter policies of not giving out any information.

When screening resumes, it helps to have your job description and specifications in front of you so you can keep the qualities and skills you are looking for clearly in mind. Because there is no standard form for resumes, evaluating them can be very subjective. However, there are certain components you should expect to find in a resume. It should contain the prospect's name, address, telephone number, and email address at the top, and a brief summary of employment and educational experience, including dates. Many resumes include a "career objective" that describes what kind of job the prospect is pursuing; other applicants state their objectives in their cover letters. Additional information you may find on a resume or in a cover letter includes references, achievements, and career-related affiliations. Many employers look closely at the "non-job" interests and activities of job candidates, especially those who are fresh out of college or grad school. Often, employers say that they were particularly impressed by candidates' extracurricular activities, from heading up organizations and mentoring and/or tutoring to athletic accomplishments that show their teamwork.

Look for neatness and professionalism in the applicant's resume and cover letter. A resume riddled with typos raises some serious red flags. If a person can't be bothered to put their best foot forward during this crucial stage of the game, how can you expect them to do a good job if hired?

Willing and Able

The Americans with Disabilities Act (ADA) of 1990 makes it illegal for employers with 15 or more employees to refuse to hire qualified people with disabilities if making "reasonable accommodations" would enable the person to carry out the duties of the job. That could mean making physical changes to the workplace or reassigning certain responsibilities.

While the law is unclear on exactly how far an employer must go to accommodate a person with disabilities, what is clear is that it's the applicant's responsibility to tell the employer about the disability. Employers are not allowed to ask whether an applicant has a disability or a history of health problems. However, after the applicant has been given a written or verbal explanation of the job duties, you may then ask whether they can adequately perform those duties or would need some type of accommodation.

For further clarification, read the laws, regulations, and enforcement guidance documents available online from the Equal Employment Opportunity Commission at eeoc.gov.

There are two basic types of resumes: the chronological resume and the functional resume. The chronological resume, which is what most of us are used to seeing, lists employment history in reverse chronological order, from the most recent position to the oldest. The functional resume does not list dates of employment; instead, it lists different skills or "functions" that the employee has performed.

Although chronological resumes are the preferred format among HR professionals and hiring managers, functional resumes have increased in popularity in recent years. In some cases, they are used by downsized executives who may be quite well qualified but unfortunately have to downplay long periods of unemployment due to a struggling economy or a career change. In some cases, however, they could signal that the applicant is a job-hopper or has something to hide.

Because it's easy for people to embellish resumes, it's a good idea to have candidates fill out a job application, online or in person, and then compare it to the resume. Because the application requires information to be completed in chronological order, it gives you a more accurate picture of an applicant's history. It might seem redundant—and sometimes candidates will naturally feel frustrated (didn't I fill this out already online?)—but it can be worth it if you use the paper application as a check-and-balance. Just make sure not to get overly detailed about dates and education—many people don't recall the date they graduated from middle school, and that's not going to make or break a candidate's success.

Beyond functional and chronological resumes, there is another type of resume that's more important to be on the lookout for. That's what one consultant calls an accomplishment versus a responsibility resume.

The responsibility resume is just that. It emphasizes the job description, saying things like "managed three account executives; established budgets; developed departmental contests." An accomplishment resume, on the other hand, emphasizes accomplishments and results, such as "cut costs by 50 percent" or "met quota every month." Such a resume tells you that the person is an achiever and has the bottom line firmly in mind.

When reading the resume, try to determine the person's career patterns. Look for steady progress and promotions in past jobs. Also look for stability in terms of length of employment. While you don't want someone who is constantly changing jobs, you need to consider that there have been three major U.S. recessions in the past 20 years: the dotcom crash of 2000, the 2008 recession, and the one caused by the COVID-19 pandemic. All these have forced people out of jobs and made it difficult to find new ones. This leads to gaps in employment and a need to change jobs, which is not the fault of the job candidate.

Be aware of how economic conditions can affect a person's resume. During a climate of frequent corporate downsizing, for example, a series of lateral career moves may signal that a person is a survivor. This also shows that the person is interested in growing and willing to take on new responsibilities even if there was no corresponding increase in pay or status. Keep in mind that just because a resume or a job application has a few gaps in it doesn't mean you should overlook it entirely. You could be making a big mistake. Stay focused on the skills and values the job applicant could bring to your company.

Off Limits

EEOC guidelines, as well as federal and state laws, prohibit asking certain questions of a job applicant, either on the application form or during the interview. What questions to sidestep? Basically, you can't ask about anything not directly related to the job, including:

- Age or date of birth (except when necessary to satisfy applicable age laws, such as: Are you over 18 years of age?)
- Sex, race, creed, color, religion, or national origin
- Disabilities of any kind
- Date and type of military discharge
- Marital status
- Maiden name (for female applicants)

Other questions to avoid:
- How many children do you have? How old are they? Who will care for them while you are at work?
- Have you ever been treated by a psychologist or a psychiatrist?
- Have you ever been treated for drug addiction or alcoholism?

- Have you ever been arrested? (You may, however, ask if the person has been convicted if it is accompanied by a statement saying that a conviction will not necessarily disqualify an applicant for employment.)
- How many days were you sick last year?
- What is your sexual orientation?
- Have you ever filed for workers' compensation? Have you ever been injured on the job?

In doubt whether a question (or comment) is offensive or not? Play it safe and zip your lip.

Interviewing Applicants

Once you've narrowed your stack of resumes to 10 or so top candidates, it's time to start setting up interviews. If you dread this portion of the process, you're not alone. Fortunately, there are some ways to put both yourself and the candidates at ease—and make sure you get all the information you need to make a smart decision. Start by preparing a list of basic interview questions in advance. While you won't read off this list like a robot, having it in front of you will ensure you cover all the bases and make sure you ask all the candidates the same questions.

The initial few moments of an interview are the most crucial. There's something to be said for first impressions. You will know quickly if candidates are confident by how they act and their level of confidence. Qualities to look for include good communication skills, a neat and clean appearance, and a friendly, cordial manner.

You can put the interviewee at ease with a bit of small talk on neutral topics. A good way to break the ice is by explaining the job and describing the company—its business, history, and future plans. Keep in mind, it's not always about you deciding on the candidate—it can also be about a good candidate with other offers deciding on your company.

Then move on to the heart of the interview. You will want to ask about several general areas, such as related experience, skills, educational training or background, and unrelated jobs. Open each area with a general, open-ended question, such as "Tell me about your last job." Avoid questions that can be answered with a "yes" or "no" or prompt obvious responses, such as "Are you detail-oriented?" Instead, ask questions that force the candidate to go into detail. The best questions are follow-up ones, such as "How did that situation come about?" or "Why did you do that?" These queries force applicants to abandon preplanned responses and dig deeper. You may also give the candidate a common situation that might come up on the job to see how they would handle it. This should be a situation that makes them think but not something overly complicated that would take some prior learning.

AHA!

Posting a position on an online job site offers you advantages like 24-hour access to job postings, unlimited text, and quick turnaround. It also allows you to screen candidates, search resume databases, and keep your ad online for a long period of time, like 30 or 60 days. Another advantage: you can typically make a change if you decide to add or alter something in the posting, which you cannot do in print.

Here are some interview questions to get you started:

- If you could design the perfect job for yourself, what would you do? Why?
- What kind of supervisor gets the best work from you?
- How would you describe your current supervisor?
- How do you structure your time?
- What are three things you like about your current job?

- What were your three biggest accomplishments in your last job? In your career?
- What can you do for our company that no one else can?
- What are your strengths/weaknesses?
- How far do you think you can go in this company? Why?
- What do you expect to be doing in five years?
- What interests you most about this company? This position?
- Describe three situations where your work was criticized—what were the issues and how did you respond?
- Have you hired people before? If so, what did you look for?

A candidate's responses will give you a window into their knowledge, attitude, and sense of humor. Watch for signs of "sour grapes" about former employers. Also be alert for areas people seem reluctant to talk about. You may be able to probe a little deeper with a simple question, but be careful you don't end up on topics that are not what you should be conversing about.

When each interview is over, file the paperwork somewhere so you can find it in case you have a need for more employees later, or someone you hire doesn't work out.

Pay attention to the candidate's nonverbal cues, too. Do they seem alert and interested, or are they checking their watch or their phone? Are their clothes wrinkled and stained or clean and neat? A person who can't make an effort for the interview certainly won't make one on the job if hired.

Family Tax Savings

Want to get good employees and tax savings, too?

Hiring family, especially children, enables you to move family income out of a higher tax bracket and into a lower one. It also enables you to transfer wealth to your kids without incurring federal gift or estate taxes.

Subject to applicable child labor laws, even preteen children can be employed. If a child's salary is reasonable, it is considered earned income and not subject to the "kiddie tax" rules that can apply to anyone under the age of 23. And if your business is unincorporated, wages paid to a child under 18 are not subject to Social Security or FICA taxes. That means neither you nor your child has to pay these taxes. Be sure to document the type of work the family member is doing and pay them a comparable amount to what you'd pay another employee, or the IRS will think you're putting your family on the payroll just for the tax breaks. Keep careful records of time worked, and make sure the work is necessary to the business.

Your accountant can suggest other ways to take advantage of this tax situation without getting in hot water.

Finally, leave time at the end of the interview for the applicant to ask questions—and pay attention to what they ask. This is the time when applicants can really show they have done their homework and researched your company or, conversely, that all they care about is what they can get out of the job. End the interview by letting the candidate know what to expect next. Let them know when they can expect to hear from you. You are dealing with other people's livelihoods, so the week that you take to finish your interviews can seem like an eternity to them. Show some consideration by keeping them informed.

During the interview, jot down notes (without being obvious about it). After the interview, allow five or 10 minutes to write down the applicant's outstanding qualities and evaluate their personality and skills against your job description and specifications.

To Test or Not to Test

Personality and skills assessments are important when screening key employees. This is especially true for sales and customer-facing jobs. According to Psychometrics, a company that leads the pack in offering personality assessments in the workplace, "Personality assessments provide a measure of how individuals work with people, approach their tasks, communicate, approach change, and deal with stress. Differences between people in these various areas can make them more or less effective in different jobs."

There are work personality assessments, skill strength assessments, career value indicators, and more. Psychometrics.com is a good place to start, although other organizations also offer the assessments and the scoring. A simple questionnaire test might cost as little as $20 to $50 per assessment. More complex assessments can cost $125 or more.

Look for tests that have highly reliable results and those that are most commonly used in your industry. If you can afford the extra cost, personality assessments can be a good extra screen to ensure your new hires have just the right temperament to sell your products, greet your customers, or stay motivated to help you get ahead. Many people interview well but might not behave the same way in person; you'd rather know this before you hire someone than after they've offended a customer.

Of course, asking candidates to take personality tests can make it harder to secure experienced prospects who have built their reputation and don't appreciate being tested. When it comes to passing judgment on how people will act (and fit in) based on random testing, you may be met with criticism and diminish your hopes of building a strong, engaged corporate culture. Moreover, if any type of testing appears to weed out people based on color, gender, ethnicity, or religion, you'll have far more problems on your hands. As you can see, unless it's strictly skills-related—which also doesn't appeal to some top prospects but may be necessary when it comes to using new technology—there are some strong reasons not to test.

Checking References

After preliminary interviews, you should be able to narrow the field to three or four top candidates. Now's the time to do a little detective work.

It's estimated that up to one-third of job applicants lie about their experience and educational achievements on their resumes or job applications. No matter how sterling the person seems in the interview process, a little online research and/or a few phone calls up-front to check out their claims could save you a lot of hassles—and even legal battles—later. Today, largely because of identity theft, getting that information has become harder and harder. Many firms have adopted policies that forbid releasing detailed information. Generally, the investigating party is referred to a personnel department, which supplies dates of employment, title, and salary—period.

You can also try calling the person's former supervisor directly. While the supervisor may be required to send you to personnel, sometimes you'll get lucky and get the person on a day they feel like talking.

Sometimes, too, a supervisor can tip you off without saying anything that will get them in trouble. Consider the supervisor who, when contacted by one potential employer, said, "I only give good references." When the employer asked, "What can you tell me about X?" the supervisor repeated, "I only give good references." Without saying anything, they said it all.

Depending on the position, you may also want to do education checks. You can call any college or university's admissions department to verify degrees and dates of attendance. Some universities will require a written request or a signed waiver from the applicant before releasing any kind of information.

If the person is going to be driving a company vehicle, you may want to check with the department of motor vehicles. In fact, you may want to do this even if they will not be driving for you. Vehicle checks can uncover patterns of negligence or potential drug and alcohol problems.

SAVE
Whenever possible, look for employees you can cross-train for different jobs. A welder with college courses in engineering and an administrative assistant with human resources experience are workers one business owner has successfully cross-trained. Cross-trained employees can fill in when others are absent, helping keep costs down.

If your company deals with property management, such as maintenance or cleaning, you may want to consider a criminal background check as well. Unfortunately, national criminal records and even state records are not coordinated. The only ways to obtain criminal records are to either go to individual courthouses in each county, or do an online search—sometimes it's for a fee, but you can find out a lot about a candidate's background if records are publicly available. It's generally sufficient to investigate records in three counties—birthplace, current residence, and residence preceding the current residence.

Research Prospective Candidates

Another common way for employers to learn more about candidates is by visiting their social media pages. It can be enlightening to look not only at a candidate's profile page, but also their posts. You may be impressed by a candidate's social media presence and end up hiring them based in part by what you read. However, you might also reject candidates if you find inappropriate posts, including discriminatory comments about gender, race, or religion; disparaging jabs about previous employers; or references to drug use or photos of partying or drinking. In some cases, you might find that an applicant's screen name is questionable, while in other instances, if someone is constantly posting, that could be a telltale sign that their social media time may cut into their job time.

By now, job candidates should know that their social media presence matters when they are job hunting. All that considered,

keep in mind that a posting by a naive 16-year-old may not represent that same individual at 25. People make mistakes and grow
up. Therefore, look for patterns or what they've posted recently.

Credit Checks

For certain positions, such as those that will give an employee
access to your company's cash (a cashier or an accounting clerk,
for instance), a credit check may be a good idea as well. You can
find credit reporting bureaus online. They will be able to provide
you with a limited credit and payment history. While you should
not rely on this as the sole reason not to hire someone (credit
reports are notorious for containing errors), a credit report can
contribute to a total picture of irresponsible behavior. And if the
person will have access to large sums of money at your company,
hiring someone who is in serious debt is probably not a good idea.

Be aware, however, that if a credit check plays any role in your
decision not to hire someone, you must inform them that they
were turned down in part because of their credit report.

If all this background checking seems too time-consuming
to handle yourself, you can contract the job out to a third-party
investigator. Google "background checking." A criminal check
can cost as little as $18; a full investigation averages $60. There
are even better deals online, so be sure to shop around. Be careful
to find a legit place. Also try to find someone who has used the
same background checking service before, or look for reviews
of the service. It's a small price to pay when you consider the
damages it might save you.

After the Hire

Congratulations! You have hired your first employee. Now what?

As soon as you hire, call or email the applicants who came in
for interviews and let them know you chose another candidate,
but you will keep their applications on file. Also, if you keep their
applications on file, you won't have to start from scratch when

hiring your second employee.

For each applicant you interviewed, create an employee file including your interview notes, their resume, and the employment application. That file will become the basis for their personnel file. Federal law requires that a job application be kept at least three years after a person is hired.

Most businesses enter all client information in their computer system. This is a convenient way to save information, but keeping hard copies is also important. When you enter candidates into the system, make sure you have passwords and firewalls set up to keep their information as safe as possible. Stories of hackers breaching companies' personnel databases abound. If you are unsure about the safety of your personnel (and other) records, hire someone with an accredited background in online security to help guide you through a process that will keep your data protected. Data security is an important issue, so this is not a place to save money by assuming your data is safe.

Even if you don't hire the applicant, make sure you keep the file. Under federal law, all recruitment materials, such as applications and resumes, must be kept for at least six months after the employment decision has been made. In today's climate, where applicants sometimes sue an employer who decides not to hire them, it's a good idea to maintain all records related to a hire (or non-hire). Especially for higher-level positions where you narrow the field to two or three candidates, put a brief note or memo in each applicant's file explaining why they were or were not hired.

Prior to your applicant's first day, if your new hire is working in an office setting, make sure you have their office or workstation set up for them to get started. People are usually enthusiastic, yet somewhat nervous, on their first day of work. It's important to build on the momentum of their motivation by having a place set up for them to work, making them comfortable and welcome. Don't just dump them in an office and shut your door. Be prepared to spend some time with them, explaining job duties, introducing them to their office mates, getting them started on tasks, showing them around, and/or even taking them out to lunch. By doing so, you are building rapport and setting the stage for a long and happy working relationship.

"I think people who have a real entrepreneurial spirit, who can face difficulties and overcome them, should absolutely follow their desires. It makes for a much more interesting life."
—Martha Stewart, founder of
Martha Stewart Living Omnimedia

Alternatives to Full-Time Employees

The traditional full-time employee is not your only hiring option. More employers are turning to alternative arrangements, including leased employees, temporary employees, part-timers, and interns. All these strategies can save you money—and headaches too.

Leasing Employees

Employee leasing is a contractual arrangement in which the leasing company, also known as a professional employer organization (PEO), is the official employer. Employee leasing lets you add workers without adding administrative complexity.

By combining the employees of several companies into one larger pool, PEOs can offer business owners better rates on healthcare and workers' compensation coverage.

Today, PEOs do a lot more than just offer better healthcare rates. They manage everything from compliance with state and federal regulations to payroll, unemployment insurance, W-2 forms, and claims processing—saving clients time and money. Some firms have even branched out to offer "extras," such as pension and employee assistance programs.

While many business owners confuse PEOs with temporary help businesses, the two organizations are quite different. Generally speaking, temporary help companies recruit employees and assign them to client businesses to help with short-term work overload or special projects on an as-needed basis, according to a spokesperson with the American Staffing Association. With PEOs, on the other hand, a client business generally turns over all its personnel functions to the outside PEO company, which will administer these operations and lease the employees back to the client.

According to NAPEO (National Association of Professional Employer Organizations), such leasing services are contractual arrangements in which the PEO is the employer of record for all or part of the client's workforce. Employment responsibilities are typically shared between the PEO and the client, allowing the client to retain essential management control over the work performed by the employees.

Meanwhile, the PEO assumes responsibility for a wide range of employer obligations and risks, among them paying and reporting wages and employment taxes out of its own accounts as well as retaining some rights to the direction and control of the leased employees. The client, on the other hand, has one primary responsibility: writing one check to the PEO to cover the payroll, taxes, benefits, and administrative fees. The PEO does the rest.

Who uses PEOs? According to NAPEO, small businesses make up the primary market because—due to economies of scale—they typically pay higher premiums for employee benefits. If an employee hurts their back and files a workers' compensation claim, it could threaten the existence of a small business. With another entity as the employer of record, however, these claims are no longer the small business owner's problem. PEOs have also been known to help business owners avoid wrongful termination suits and negligent acts in the workplace, according to an NAPEO spokesperson.

Having to comply with a multitude of employment-related statutes, which is often beyond the means of smaller businesses, is another reason PEOs are so popular with entrepreneurs. According to NAPEO, with a PEO you basically get the same type of human resources department you would get if you were a Fortune 500 firm.

Look before You Lease

How do you decide if an employee leasing company is for you? The National Association of Professional Employer Organizations (NAPEO) suggests you look for the following:

- Services that fit your human resources needs. Is the company flexible enough to work with you?
- Banking and credit references. Look for evidence that the company's payroll taxes and insurance premiums are up-to-date. Request to see a certificate of insurance.
- Investigate the company's administrative competence. What experience does it have?
- Understand how employees' benefits are funded. Do they fit your workers' needs? Find out who the third-party administrator or carrier is and whether it is licensed if your state requires this.
- Make sure the leasing company is licensed or registered if required by your state.
- Ask for client and professional references, and call them.
- Review the agreement carefully and try to get a provision that permits you to cancel on short notice—say, 30 days.

For a list of NAPEO member organizations in your area, you can search their resources and directory online at napeo.org, email them at info@napeo.org, or call them at (703) 836-0466.

Today, more than 3.7 million employees are working through PEOs. Among the leading PEOs as of 2020 are Oasis (oasisadvantage.com), TriNet (trinet.com), Justworks (justworks.com), Insperity (insperity.com), and ADP TotalSource (adp.com). If you do a Google search of PEO service providers, you will find others in your area.

Before hiring a professional employer organization, be sure to shop around because not all offer the same pricing structures and services. Fees may be based on a modest percentage of payroll (typically, three to eight percent) or on a per-employee basis. When comparing fees, consider what you would pay a full-time employee to handle the administrative chores the PEO will take off your hands.

> **WARNING**
> Be sure you understand the precise legal relationship between your business and a leasing company. Some people consider the leasing company the sole employer, effectively insulating the client from legal responsibility. Others consider the client and the leasing company joint employers, sharing legal responsibility. Have an attorney review your agreement to clarify any risks.

Temporary Employees

You may need help on a temporary basis at various times. For example, you may find yourself understaffed at a busy time of year, or perhaps you have a big sale coming up at a retail location, or your company is holding a special event and needs more people than you have on staff to plan and run everything. In other cases, you may have a seasonal business that requires you to ramp up production and/or sales during certain months of the year. Temporary help no longer means just bringing in administrative assistants; there are many types of temp employees with a wide range of skills and experience.

Today, many companies that supply temporary help specialize in medical services; others find their niche in professional or technical fields, supplying everything from temporary engineers, editors, and accountants to computer programmers, bankers, lab support staff, and even attorneys.

With many temporary help companies now offering specialized employees, business owners have learned that they don't have to settle for low skill levels or imperfect matches. Because most temporary help companies screen—and often train—their employees, entrepreneurs who choose this option stand a better chance of obtaining the quality employees they need.

In addition to prescreened, pretrained individuals, temporary help companies offer entrepreneurs a slew of other benefits. For one, they help keep your overhead low. For another, they save you time and money on recruiting efforts. You don't have to find, interview, or relocate workers. Also, the cost of health and unemployment benefits, workers' compensation insurance, profit sharing, vacation time, and other benefits doesn't come out of your budget because many temporary help companies provide these resources to their employees.

How do you find the temporary help company that best suits your needs—from light word processing to specialized technical support? First, look online for "temporary employment agencies near me," then look at some of the websites of companies to see if they provide employees with the skills you need. Once you find temporary employment agencies with people who can benefit your business, email or call a few and ask some questions, including:

- How do you handle sourcing, screening, and selecting your staffers? Do you do background checks?
- Can I review the background of some of your temporary employees?
- How much time in advance do I need to request temporary help?
- How do you handle situations that do not work out?
- Do you carry insurance? (Look for adequate liability and workers' compensation coverage to protect your company

from a temporary worker's claim.)
- Do you check on the progress of your temporary employees?
- What kind of training do you give temporaries? (According to the American Staffing Association, nearly 90 percent of the temporary work force receives free skills training of some kind.)
- What benefits do you offer?

Also ask the company to provide references. Contact references and ask their opinions of the quality level, reliability, reputation, service, and training of the temporary help agency.

Temporary Treatment

How do you make the most of your temporary workers once they've come onboard? For one, don't treat them differently from your other employees. Introduce them to your full-time workers as people who are there to help you complete a project, to relieve some overtime stress, or to bring in some skills you might not have in-house.

Don't expect temporary workers to be so well-trained that they know how to do all the little things in your office, such as operating the copier or answering the phone. Take a few minutes before they arrive and make a short list of what you need to tell them to get them started. This includes anything from passwords and office rules to where the bathrooms are and recommendations of where to get lunch. Then spend some time giving them a brief overview of these things just as you would any new employee. You might also take a minute to fill them in on the company's culture.

One strategy for building a better relationship with your temporary workers is to plan ahead as much as possible so you can use the same temporaries for an extended period—say, six months. Or try to get the same temporaries back when you need help again. This way, they'll be more productive, and you won't have to spend time retraining them. It helps if you take some notes (for yourself) on what they did well.

Defining the expected duration of your needs is also important. While many entrepreneurs bring on a temporary worker for just that—temporary work—some may eventually find they would like to hire the worker full time. Be aware that, at this point, some temporary help firms require a negotiated fee for "stealing" the employee away from them. Defining your needs up-front can help you avoid such penalties.

Because a growing number of entrepreneurs purposely use temporary workers part time to get a feel for whether they should hire them full time, many temporary help companies have begun offering an option: temporary-to-full-time programs, which allow the prospective employer and employee to evaluate each other. Temporary-to-full-time programs match a temporary worker who has expressed an interest in full-time work with an employer who has like interests. Should the match seem like a good one, the client is encouraged to make a job offer to the employee within a predetermined period.

Last but not least, before contracting with a temporary help company, make sure it is a member of a trade association, such as the American Staffing Association. This means: (1) the company has agreed to abide by a code of ethics and good practices; (2) it is in the business for the long haul, meaning it has invested in its industry by becoming a member of its trade association; and (3) it has access to up-to-date information on trends that impact its business.

FYI

Need to find an employee for your specific industry? Try a trade association's website, many of which have classified sections or job boards. These sites allow you to post job listings at a low cost and receive responses from a targeted pool of candidates.

Part-Time Personnel

Many people are looking for part-time jobs, and they can be beneficial to your needs as well. By using permanent part-timers, you can get more commitment than you'd get from a temp and more flexibility than you can get from full-timers. In some industries, such as fast food, retail, and other businesses that are open long hours, part-timers are essential to fill the odd hours during which workers are needed.

A traditional source of part-time employees is students. They typically are flexible, willing to work odd hours, and do not require high wages. High school and college kids like employers who let them fit their work schedule to the changing demands of school.

Although students are ideal for many situations, there are potential drawbacks. For one thing, a student's academic and social demands may impinge on your scheduling needs.

Students are not the only part-timers in town, however. One often overlooked source of employees is retired or semiretired people. Often, seniors are looking for a way to earn some extra money or fill their days. Many of these people have years of valuable business experience that could be a boon to your company.

Seniors offer many of the advantages of other part-time employees. They typically have an excellent work ethic and can add a note of stability to your organization.

Parents of younger children also offer a qualified pool of potential part-time workers. Often, these workers are highly skilled and experienced but might only be able to work during school hours or desire to work a limited schedule.

The Intern Alternative

Some colleges encourage students to work, for a small stipend or even for free, through internship programs. Student interns trade their time and talents in exchange for learning marketable job skills. Every year, colleges match thousands of students with businesses of all sizes and types.

Because they have an eye on future career prospects, the students are usually highly motivated.

Does your tiny one-person office have anything to offer an intern? Actually, small companies offer better learning experiences for interns since they typically involve a greater variety of job tasks and offer a chance to work more closely with senior employees.

Routine admin or "gofer" work won't get you an intern in most cases. Colleges expect their interns to learn specialized professional skills. Hold up your end of the bargain by providing meaningful work. For example, do you need someone to help with your social media marketing? College students spend a tremendous amount of time on social media. They can learn how to handle the social media needs of a business and, if they really excel at it, they can work their way into a full-time job.

Check with your local college or university to find out about internship programs. Usually, the school will send you an application and ask you to describe the job's responsibilities and your needs in terms of skill level and other qualifications. Then the school will send you resumes of students who may work for you.

The best part of hiring interns? If you're lucky, you'll find a gem who will stay with your company after the internship is over. Many universities and community colleges report that interns get hired more than half the time when an employer has an appropriate opening. This is a good indication that you'll find some great talent this way.

It can actually be in your best interest to train interns through an internship program. Like having your own minor league system, you can bring in interns to do a job, and if they respond well and show an interest, you can start training them for a position in your company. There are instances of interns working for a couple of summers or even holiday vacations at the same company, learning the ropes, and landing a job when they finish college. This can save you time and money when it comes to finding candidates for positions. In essence, you can bring in people who know how things are done and are anxious to grow in your company. By providing meaningful work experience and having a job that they can aspire to, you can turn an internship into a career.

People with disabilities also make up a strong pool of part-time employees. You can recruit employees with disabilities through local disability-related advocacy organizations in your community or through places like the Workforce Recruitment Program at wrp.gov.

The Employee Assistance and Resource Network on Disability Inclusion at askearn.org, the National Disability Institute at nationaldisabilityinstitute.org, and YAI at yai.org are also places to find more information about hiring employees with disabilities.

Contract Only What You Need

Many people today have opted to use their skills as freelancers or independent contractors. Numerous online resources can help you locate freelancers, including RemoteWorkHub.com, FlexJobs.com, Upwork.com, Guru.com, Freelancer.com, and Freelancermap.com (for IT projects). LinkedIn or even Craigslist can also be helpful in connecting skilled independent workers with businesses that have specific needs. These websites generally allow you to advertise for or search profiles of people for hire, and freelancers can advertise their rates or negotiate a rate.

Independent contractors can be a good alternative to temporary workers or to fill in a knowledge gap. Say you need someone to refine your marketing materials or handle the books for just one product. You might only have 10 hours of work per week, and you need someone with specific knowledge or skills. These sites connect you with people who specialize in all sorts of work but want to do it on their own time or prefer to pick and choose projects rather than work for one employer. In return, you might find a better rate, with fewer employment law worries, than you would at a temporary agency.

Like any hiring, review the potential candidate's work and check references. And remember, if you are paying $10 an hour for a job that should pay $20 or $30, you might not get the same quality. Remember the old saying: "You get what you pay for."

Outsourcing Options

Simply put, this refers to sending certain job functions outside your company instead of handling them in-house. For instance, instead of hiring an in-house bookkeeper, you might outsource the job to an independent bookkeeper who comes in once a month or does all the work off-site.

More and more companies, large and small, are turning to outsourcing to cut payroll and overhead costs. Done right, outsourcing can mean you never need to hire an employee.

How to make it work? Make sure the company or individual you use can do the job. That means getting (and checking) references. Ask former or current clients about their satisfaction. Find out what industries and what type of workload the firm or individual is used to handling. Can you expect your deadlines to be met, or will your smaller projects get pushed aside if a bigger client has an emergency?

Make sure you feel comfortable with the individual(s) who will be doing the work and that you can discuss your concerns and needs openly. Ask to see work samples if appropriate (for example, if you're using a graphic design firm).

If your outsourcing needs are handled by an individual, you're dealing with an independent contractor. The IRS has stringent rules regulating exactly who is and is not considered an independent contractor. The risk: if you consider a person an independent contractor and the IRS later reclassifies them as an employee, you could be liable for that person's Social Security taxes and a wide range of other costs and penalties.

If you're in doubt, it always pays to consult your accountant and/or check with IRS.gov to see how they define an independent contractor versus an employee. Making a mistake in this area could cost you big.

Index

ENJOY ENTREPRENEUR QUICK
GUIDE: CREATING, PLANNING, AND
FUNDING YOUR NEW BUSINESS?

MAKE SURE TO GRAB A COPY OF THE
NEXT BOOK IN THE SERIES:

Entrepreneur Quick Guide: Building, Marketing, and Scaling Your New Business

LEARN MORE:
ENTREPRENEUR.COM/BOOKSTORE

Printed in the USA
CPSIA information can be obtained
at www.ICGtesting.com
JSHW050750270224
58109JS00002B/2